YOUNG & LIVING FOR GOD

WWW.YOUNGANDLIVINGFORGOD.COM

KAROLYNE ROBERTS

Table of Contents

PART 1:

All About Purpose

INTRODUCTION: The Knowing Game

Before you read anything else in this book, you should know that, I don't know everything. I know that I don't know everything and it's that same "not knowing everything" that has allowed God to move mightily in my life. You see, us humans "know" too much—or at least we think we do. The most important thing that I will ever know is that God is all knowing and His word is true. Everything else is simply "up for grabs" meaning He can take it away and replace it with something new. You may be familiar with the name of that process; it is call "the renewal of the mind". The bible says in Romans 12:2, "And be not conformed to this world: but be transformed by the renewing of your mind, that you may prove what is that good, and acceptable, and perfect, will of God."

I am 21-years-young and living out God purpose and will for my life. It is not because I know-it-all! It's simply because from a young age, I've learned how to say, "Lord I don't know everything. Have your way. Not my will Lord, but let your will be done." That's what God loves about the youth today. I am not talking about a select age range; I mean the youth at heart. I am talking about those who are young in spirit. I am talking about those who are not necessarily marked by immaturity but humility—the meek. I am talking about the one's who have submitted themselves to the leading of the Holy Spirit; surrendered themselves to a life of faith. The bible says in Mathew 18:3, "And he said: 'Truly I tell you, unless you change and become like little children, you will never enter the Kingdom of heaven.'" Here, Jesus was not talking about transforming in physically terms, but he was talking about the attitude of our spirits. We should be like children, slow to speak and quick to listen. (James 1:19)

These kinds of people don't have to know everything, they don't have to see and understand every last detail. They have a sixth sense, and it's not natural, but spiritual. They have abandoned all that they know and have decided to trust God. "Trust in the LORD with all your heart; and lean not unto your own understanding; in all your ways acknowledge Him and He shall direct your paths" (Proverbs 3:5-6). What does it mean to "acknowledge Him?" Well in other versions, this word is replaced with *know*. To acknowledge God is to know Him and have a relationship with Him. It means to actually talk to Him in prayer, spend time in His presence, and do things that make Him happy just because you love Him. It means to keep His commandments. The bible says in 1 John 2:3-5 says: "And by this we know that we know Him, if we keep His commandments. He that says, I know Him, and keeps not His commandments, is a liar, and the truth is not in Him. But whoever keeps His word, in Him verily is the love of God perfected: by this we know that we are in Him." That means that, it's impossible to know God truly, to be that intimate with Him and experience Him, and not be changed forever. There is no Love like the Love of God's. He is Love.

The best way to read the rest of this book is to abandon everything you think you know and continually ask yourself this question: *Do I know God?*

Do you know Him? My prayer is that, by the end of this book, *you will*. Then *you will* be able to go and live out God's perfect will for your life.

PRAYER:

Daddy, I thank you for this day. I thank you for meeting me through this book in Your perfect timing. I thank You for knowing where I am and still loving me as I am. Father God, please help me abandon everything I know so that I can know You more. God, apart from You I am nothing and a part from You, I have nothing. Be my everything starting today. If You are willing, please show and confirm my purpose through this book. I want to live a life of faith and I want Your desires to be mine. Lord, remove from within me anything that is unlike you. Create in me a clean heart, and renew a right spirit within me. Lord, I forgive those in my past who have hurt me. I let go of those situations that I don't understand. I let go of all the things that made me question your sovereignty and character. Lord, teach me how to love you. Give me the grace to be obedient to your word because your word says that all things happen for the good of those who love you, and who are called according to your purpose. Daddy, please turn my mess into a message, for Your Glory and Yours alone. Have your way Lord. In Jesus' name I pray, Amen.

I Don't know My Purpose!

Ok, on the count of three take a deep breath: One.....Two.....and Three.....BREATHEEEEE! Thank you. So, you may not know your purpose. Well guess what, it's not the end of the world! As long as you *know* God, you are in purpose. It's not by coincidence you are reading this book right now, whether you know why or not. God knows... and if you're living that life of faith that we talked about, that should be enough for you. You don't have to know everything right away. Maybe God just wants you to trust Him, and in His perfect time He will reveal. Some of the people reading this book may already know their purpose, some may discover it from reading this book, and some may read this book and still not have a clue. The good news about that is: God is in CONTROL. We are in different places in life. Why? Honestly I don't know. God has His way of timing things. I can guess a million reasons but I still may land on the wrong answer every time. God works in mysterious ways.

Here are my guesses (just for fun): People who know God early, probably have people in their lives who need to be saved REALLY soon. So they must know their purpose now so that they can influence certain people before they leave the earth. Or maybe those same people would've given up on trying to know God because it seemed like it was taking forever for them to realize their purpose, so God showed them their purpose early so that He could save them form never knowing Him. Maybe people who know God late have a purpose that requires a lot of responsibility so they have to go through years or training and tests before God reveals to them their purpose. If God had revealed their purpose to them on day one, they may have been overwhelmed by it's greatness and would've given up. Or maybe you may never know your purpose because your purpose may have nothing to do with your life on earth, but may have everything to do with the way you die. Maybe you weren't put here to be an example for this generation, but for the next. If God revealed to you your purpose right know, you may be scared out of your wits. Remember, fear does not come from God but God knows everything so I bet you He knows some very scary information, but He will never tell us something that would instill a spirit of fear within us. Fear is from the devil; so if you ever feel fearful, cast that spirit out immediately. The bible says: "For God has not given us a spirit of fear; but of power, and of love, and of a sound mind" (2 Timothy 1:7).

Before you know your purpose, God will send tests and trials your way to instill His power within you. You will get stronger and stronger and you will need that strength to carry out His will for your life. You will be hurt, you may even get heart broken, but you will learn forgiveness and you will learn love, and as Christians, we all need to learn how to love to truly reflect the life of Jesus. You will gain a sound mind. You will learn faith and learn how to trust God even when you don't understand and know. After He has built up those character traits in you, and when He decides that it's time to reveal your purpose… be sure to not let everything you learned in those years go out the window and don't leave room for fear. Of course we will have moments of fear that will come knocking at our door, especially when we feel inadequate to do what God has called us to do, but we should not let fear paralyze us. Fear is not a family member, but only a guest that was sent by the enemy…its visitation should always be short, but love, power, and peace, those were *given* to us by God. They are members of our family and a part of our spiritual DNA.

Your purpose is in knowing God. Your purpose is in keeping His commandments and walking like Jesus walked. If you do this, you will be living in purpose before you even know it. Remember, God made you ON purpose. You are not a mistake! Even if your parent's thought you were, God had you planned all along and they were just vessels used to bring you forth. Jeremiah 1:5 says: "Before I formed you in the womb I knew you, before you were born I set you apart; I appointed you as a prophet to the nations." Stop spending your sweet time and money on coaching programs and mentors that are "leading you to find purpose." People know what you crave and they'll exploit that desire and use it against you. Spend fifty bucks on a bible and you'll do a better job at finding your purpose there. If anyone knows your purpose, it's not Sally Sue's pastor around the corner—it's God. You want to know something else? He's with you WHEREVER you go. He is omniscient, as a matter of fact; He is hovering over you RIGHT NOW. I know it may sound stalkerish, but get this; God is crazy in love with you!

Your Desire to Matter

Please stop stressing about everything you don't know, because even if you knew your purpose, and every piece of knowledge and wisdom on the face of this earth, but did not know God, nothing would be *worth* knowing. Only God is *worth* knowing. Everything else is meaningless and in due season will fade away. God is eternal. 1st Corinthians 3: 18-20 says: "Let no one deceive himself. If anyone among you seems to be wise in this age, let him become a fool that he may become wise. For the wisdom of this world is foolishness with God. For it is written, "He catches the wise in their *own* craftiness"; and again, "The Lord knows the thoughts of the wise, that they are futile."

You see, here's what happens when you get a little "glimpse" of your purpose, a word from the prophet, and you think you have it all-figured-out—you get crafty! Just like it says in the scripture, "He catches the wise in their own craftiness." You just have a little idea of what God call you to do so know you try to make it happen by yourself because you don't want to feel like you're crazy. You don't fully trust God and you'd hate to think that you have *voices* in your head so you manipulate your life, you connections, and your "opportunities" into looking like the word that your received from *God*. You don't trust God to finish what He started so you take matters into your own hands. You ran around telling everyone, "this is my purpose, God gave me a vision, and this is what He revealed to me!" And now that everything around you doesn't necessarily look like what God said, you try to *prove* to everyone that you're not crazy.

Listen, the point of your purpose is not so that you can prove anything to anybody! It's not so that you can show people that you have *value*. As a matter of fact, your purpose has absolutely nothing to do with you. Your purpose is about what God is trying to do through you, for everyone else. Toilet paper has purpose, but the purpose of the toilet paper is not for the toilet paper. The purpose of the toilet paper is to serve others.

"God show me my purpose, I want to know my purpose!" Are you ready to serve? Are you ready to be that toilet paper? No, really? Are you ready for God to send you into the dirtiest and smelliest places of men, and to be used by Him to wipe them clean? Or, are you just asking God for your purpose because you want to feel validated? You want to *prove* to someone that you have a reason to be here—just because, *you want to matter*. Listen, you got to get the point where you understand that you do matter, even when you don't know your purpose. If you don't, you will make your *desire to matter*, matter more than you, and the enemy will take that desire as bait, and use that to reel you in. He'll make you *feel* like you matter, in exchange for your soul, but be careful, feelings are only temporary. He'll make you feel important, on top of the world; he'll give you exactly what you want… *your desire to matter*. You may have all the fame in the world, cars that good money can buy, the applause and approval from men and to the world you may matter, but inside you'll still feel empty and broken. Your value was never supposed to come from them, your value was supposed to come from Jesus Christ. Your value was determined over 2,000 years ago, when God came down as man, to pay the price for your sins. He gave the gift of grace that we never deserved, and sealed the promise by filling us with His Holy spirit when we chose to accept this precious gift of salvation. You are not cheap. Not even purpose can afford to pay the price of what you are worth. Even if you had no purpose at all, even if God decided to make you—just because He felt like it, you'd be valuable. You are not valuable because of what defines you. You are valuable because the living God, the Alpha and Omega, the beginning and the end, the Creator of the universe, loved you so much, that He sent His one and only son to die for your sins so that if you believed in Him, you would not perish but have everlasting life! (John 3:16)

If you go so hard chasing after your purpose, rather than chasing after God, the enemy will quench your thirst, by giving you purpose, in his own will. I don't know about you, but I rather rest and remain in purpose to carry out God's plan for my life than be moved by worldly ambition and be in purpose to carry out the enemy's plan for my life. They both have a plan...make sure you're living in the right one.

That is why you have to be careful with your desires. The same way we have to disregard all that we know and renew are minds when we want to know God, is the same way we have to abolish our desires. Our natural desires are evil, because we are all born without knowing God. We need to go through the process or exchanging our desires for God's desires, and eventually, His desires will be what we desire to. It's the process of being in peace and harmony with our Lord and King, or becoming one with Him. It's the process of growing in contentment, and realizing that He's enough. Just like a man and a woman become one when they are married, we become a part of the body of Christ when we get saved—we are His bride. Meaning, we should have His mind, we should think like Him, walk like Him, and talk like Him. The bible says in Psalm 37:4, "Delight yourself in the LORD; And He will give you the desires of your heart." Many times when people read this scripture they think, "yes! God wants me to prosper! God will give me whatever I want!" Let's get something straight here; God is God, not Santa Claus. I'm sorry to burst your bubble but He is not here to fulfill your perfect plan, we are here to fulfill His. The previous verse was originally written in the Hebrew, and translated in the Hebrew, the word "delight" means: to be pliable or sensitive, to be dependent upon God and to derive one's pleasures from Him. So to delight in the Lord, means to be in the position to be *molded* by Him. This means you are ready for change and you are *sensitive* to His Holy Spirit. When you delight in the Lord that means you are fully lead by Him. You don't move unless He says move, and you don't talk unless He says speak. You don't chase your desires and your own worldly ambitions. You are constrained because of your love for Him. Your pleasures come from Him because your pleasure is Him! To truly delight in Him means to share His desires and desire to please Him.

I Can't Do it Alone

I could have chosen to write this book on my own but this one is different. You see, it's not about me. I am not writing this book so that you have a distanced view of me. This book is not meant to make you feel inferior, or any less than I am or than you are. The truth is, I am nothing without God, and the same God I serve, will be in you if you accept Him and truly believe in Him with all your heart.

Nothing I have accomplished in life is new. Everything I've done has been done and repeated under the sun. What is new, is my experiences. God created me in His image, and I once heard a wise man say that I am God's newest idea; we all are. That being said, though some of us may share similar gifts, and carry the same message, we should never think that our operating in them is in vain. When we give our gifts to God, and connect our message to His will and purpose, God can make a new thing, and a good thing, out of anything.

So you, yes you, what's new about you? What's unique about you? I challenge you to find it throughout reading this book but remember; you won't find it from you. What people have you met? What experiences have you had? In what ways have you thought about those people and those experiences? All those answers, accumulated into one, are a reflection of your unique life and who you are as a person.

Do not let anything that is holding you back, define you. You are product of your own permission. Do not give yourself permission to be any less than you are because you are made in the image of God. In Him, there are no limitations. So why do you let people's opinions about who you are or the enemy's lies about your identity, frame your perspective of yourself? Do not accept that. Do not let people, or even *spirits*, make silly little affirmations over your life; cast down every attack with the word of God. Words are powerful. What you say has the power and influence to define you, and to define the world around you.

When people hear about my accomplishments, one of the most common questions that I'm always asked is, "How old are you?" When I respond, "21", I don't always get the "Wow, you're doing so great at such a young age." Sometimes I get the, "Why are you rushing life?" "Why don't you just be a kid?" or my favorite, "Wow, you're just a baby." I couldn't care less whether or not people compliment me for my age or works, but the glory is God's.

I also do not care how much people try to dumb me down or belittle me because of my young age. I understand that their own insecurities about what I am doing in my life and my decision to live boldly for Christ, has absolutely nothing to do with me. So I simply respond, "Yes, I'm young and living for God, and I love it." This is who I am. I will not let anyone try to tell me who I am and make it negative, but I will cherish who I am at this and at any other moment in my life, and make it positive. When I'm old, my desire is that, I don't sit around and sulk about my life that's passed, but still dedicate my whole being and perspective to serving God. If my future grand children or anyone ever says, "Grandma, you're getting old"... my heart is to say, "Yes, very old. I've been living for God all these years. I am a forerunner in getting ready to see my Almighty King!"

So what about you? What have you been letting people speak into your life? Well, I'm hoping this book will help to revert any discouragement you've ever received about your identity and your age. Age is a product of time, and because time is a man-made concept, because God is an eternal God, it is safe to say that it's a construct built from fear so people associate fear with age as well. Yet, you don't have to be fearful. The Bible says that: "God hath not given us a spirit of fear; but of power, and love, and of a sound mind" (2 Timothy 1:7). So I do not fear time, or my age as I grow through life, but I love it, I power through it, and I am able to think clearly of who I really am.

Like I said earlier, this is not about me. I wrote this book with the help of many young contributing writers, who are living their lives for God as well. I needed their help so that you can see that I am not the only young person who God is using to be a light and inspiration in the earth realm. There are youth all across this world just like you and me that are living this out day by day! They have joined in with me on this assignment to help empower and equip you to be a Godly leader in this day and age.

You may wonder, why is this so important? My brothers and sisters, you are tomorrow, and today isn't looking so bright. If you thought you didn't have a purpose, today, I am here to tell you otherwise. You may not know it, but look around you, pay attention. We are in the final hour. We live in a world where the name of God is banned in our schools, but teachers freely announce their bisexuality to the whole school. We live in a world where Christians are being beheaded for confessing their faith, where our very own nation is turning against Israel, God's land, and innocent people are dying every day as a result of harassment and negligence from the armed forces. Christians are being killed and persecuted all across the globe. Martial law is here, and very slowly, the rights of American citizens are being taken away to fulfill this new world order. If you don't believe me, I don't know what to tell you –Google it.

God has given me this great task of writing this book to equip you, young adults and youth, for this final hour both spiritually and physically. I did not hold anything back from this book. I know and am believing that from this, some of you will start businesses, others will write books, some will even go across the world to a far county to proclaim the gospel of Jesus Christ. Please do not take this great commission lightly. You may have been waiting for a sign, but the very fact that you are reading this book is no coincidence. You have been called by God to live an extraordinary life. You have been called by God to shake things up in this world and lead others to Christ.

It's a big fight. There is a war going on and you may not even know it but I'm here to tell you about it today. God is at war with the enemy for your soul. It is not that the enemy is as powerful as God, the enemy has no power at all when it comes to God but the power from God lies within you. That means you have a decision to make. God will not force you to serve Him. The war for your soul is a race to see whom you will accept into your heart, which you will choose. God is a gentlemen and He gives us free will. If you choose death, that is your choice. If you choose life, that is your choice.

"This day I call the heavens and the earth as witnesses against you that I have set before you life and death, blessings and curses. Now choose life, so that you and your children may live" –Deuteronomy 30:19

This war is serious. The enemy wants to distract your from your purpose so He uses "fun" to take you away from God. He doesn't want you to know God. He may have you in the club every weekend, or may have your ears budded with music and songs that don't glorify God. He may have you trapped in unhealthy relationships that distract you because other people have become your god, or you may be drowned in your own ambitions to make money, be successful, get a degree, or whatever else. Not that all those things are bad, but the enemy likes to take good things and put them in a context that displeases God. Whenever something distracts us from fulfilling our purpose, or whenever something becomes an idol, and we give it worship and attention that should be given to God, it's a sin.

Before you can go on to do amazing things like these youth are doing in this book, you have to accept Jesus as your personal Lord and savior. Anyone can become successful in life, according to the world's terms but real success is not just gaining the whole world. Real success is obedience to God, as my Pastor Cornelius Lindsey puts it. Having Real success only happens when you keep God first and realize that it is only through Him that we can do the unimaginable, the miraculous.

"What good is it for someone to gain the whole world, yet forfeit their soul?"

- Mark 8:36

If you have not yet accepted Jesus into your life, as your personal savior, you can do you so now. The Bible says, "If you declare with your mouth, "Jesus is Lord," and believe in your heart that God raised him from the dead, you will be saved." (Romans 10:9)

Keep in mind that for this confession to actually work, you have to live it. Your life must be an open confession of your belief and there should be a very clear transformation of your character. Jesus died for you. He took all the sins of the world on His back, even yours. Don't let the enemy tell you you're not good enough. Don't let Him tell you that you don't deserve God's love. It is all just another lying tactic to keep you away from God who is loving and forgiving. He doesn't care about your past, as long as you repent and turn your life over to Him.

"Come now and let us reason together, says the LORD, though your sins are like scarlet, they shall be as white as snow; though they are red like crimson, they shall be as wool." –Isaiah 1:18

"For as the heavens are high above the earth, so great is His mercy toward those who fear Him; as far as the east is from the west, so far has He removed our transgressions from us." –Psalms 103:11-12

He loves you so much. Are you ready for His return? We have a world full of people to turn back to Him. I am calling you on a mission with me, to become the bold and Godly leaders we need to be in order to pull people out of the darkness, and into eternal life. This is *your* call to action! This is what it means to be *Young and Living for God.*

PART 2:

Empowering You to Live in Purpose

YOU CAN **SHARE THE GOSPEL**

The gospel is a message meant for everyone to share, and everyone to hear. Though I do not believe that everyone is called to be a preacher, I do believe that everyone has the capability of sharing the word of God. Why would God limit the sharing of the gospel only to preachers? He wouldn't. He wouldn't because there are some parts of this world where you won't find a preacher, or a church for miles. Everyday Christians have a responsibility to share the gospel, just as much as any other leader in the church. God has assigned certain souls to your life. Some people in this would are divinely connected to you and you need to do your part so that they can be in line with God's purpose for their own life.

When the Holy Spirit whispers to you and says, "Go tell my daughter I love her, tell her about the cross." What is your initial response? Do you think: *She's going to think I'm weird* or *I won't make any friends if people hear me talk about Jesus?* Thoughts like that are from the enemy. He knows that if he can keep you from obeying God and sharing the truth of the gospel, he has another opportunity to take a soul to hell, to drag them to the place where there is weeping and gnashing of teeth.

What would you do if the next day that person died and you did not tell them about Jesus? Or what if that person was a close friend of family member? There is nothing you can do. I am not trying to scare you but I just want you to realize how serious this is. When you share the gospel with others, sometimes it may *feel* like you're being a burden but your feelings are only temporary. What about the spirit realm? Don't let the natural things of this world rule you. A burden in the natural is many times a blessing in the spiritual. The person you share the gospel with may not see it now, but later down the road, wherever they end up, they will eventually realize that what you shared with them was truth. Hopefully, they remember you when they're standing in God's glorious presence, rather than burning in hell's eternal flames.

Do not listen to the enemy if He tells you that you're not saved enough, not spiritual enough, not versed enough to share Jesus. We are all growing. We will never be saved enough, but just saved, never spiritual enough, but just spiritual, and so on. You can't put a cap on the spirit. God is so big and eternal; we have room to grow past the ends of this earth and beyond.

God has blessed us with many skills and many gifts. These skills are connected to our capability to do things; and gifts, our calling to do things. I have the skill of cooking good meals so that I can feed my family healthy food. Skills are needed to survive in this world. My skill of cooking may be something that helps my family survive naturally, but the skill of sharing the gospel is so that I can help people in this world survive spiritually. Just because I have this skill does not mean I am a preacher. I have the gift of teaching, because that is a part of my calling. Teaching is more than a skill that I have to help myself or others survive. Teaching is connected to the specific assignment I have been instructed to complete on the earth.

Though very different, both skills and gifts are important. Skills can be used to benefit situations and people in specific moments. Gifts are used to bring glory to God out of a lifetime and unite the body of Christ. As Christians, every one of us, if not all, has encountered an unbeliever at some point in time. As born again believers, we should have the basic skills, based on the character of Christ, needed to show someone love and compassion, and even possibly lead them to salvation. We should all have these basic characteristics, regardless of what our gifts are.

As a Christian, God gave you the skill of sharing the gospel so that you can give a word to the person who is having a rough day on your job. He gave you skills for that moment when you witness to someone who has just been shot in front of you, so that you can lead them to salvation in their last moments, though no one's there. He gave you those skills for your dying parent who refused to ever go to church. We were all given these skills, these characteristics, these basic attributes, as Christians because we are a part of the body, and those who have gifts, though they reach many, can't always reach everyone.

There is this widely accepted idea that because we have gifts in the body of Christ, everyone needs to "stay in his or her lane" but this theory is unbiblical and untrue. In 1st Corinthians, the Bible makes it clear many times that we are one "one spirit." That means that we are all connected into one flow of power. We flow into each other because though we've been given different gifts, we haven't been given different spirits. 1 Corinthians 12:4 says, "Now there are diversities of gifts, but the same Spirit." The apostle Paul, the author of this book of the Bible, chose to say this for a specific reason. During the time, the Church of Corinth to which he was writing had many divisions and confusions about the roles to be played in the church. In 1st Corinthians 1:10, Paul tells the Corinthians, "Now I plead with you, brethren, by the name of our Lord Jesus Christ, that you all speak the same thing, and that there be no divisions among you, but that you be perfectly joined together in the same mind and in the same judgment."

Therefore, if it is God's intention for us to be united, and if we are intertwined into one flow of the Spirit besides our unique gifts, we have an undeniable role to play alongside each other's specialties. Simply put, we need each other. The preacher, though he may travel the world and speak to thousands of people at a time, he is only one man, and may never be able to reach your neighbor next door. That is why though it may not be the mantle upon your life; God has given you the skills to operate purposefully in every area of your life, not just in the areas you are gifted in.

If we go further to 1st Corinthians 12:21-22, we see that it says, "And the eye cannot say unto the hand, I have no need of thee: nor again the head to the feet, I have no need of you. Nay, much more those members of the body, which seem to be more feeble, are necessary." We are the body, with many different parts, but one part can't say to another "I don't need you." We need each other to successfully carry out God's plan. It even says that those members of the body who seem less honorable, those who are behind the scenes, those who don't get the credit and many times never get to experience the fame or honor for their good deeds, those people are the most necessary. They are needed. Do not think because you have some weaknesses, a stuttering problem, a shameful past, awkward social skills, that God can't use you to preach His word. God can use anyone!

He used Moses to free the Israelites from Egyptian slavery, to lead them to the promise land. Moses had a speaking impediment, but that did not stop him from being used by God. God can use you, to preach, to do anything.

I started preaching during my eleventh grade year in high school. I was not ready for the platform I had, but I was placed in the position. That year, I had recently gotten saved, and started at a new church. I was getting closer to God, reading my Bible often, and becoming involved in my church. I had just gotten out of a verbally abusive relationship and I was dealing with the shame I still felt from it. I was ashamed of my sexually immoral habits with my boyfriend, sending him degrading pictures of myself through the phone, and sneaking out to hang out with him on weeknights. I was not ready to be a preacher.

Now, don't get me wrong. At that time, I was so excited to talk about God. He saved me from my horrible relationship and all things were new, even though they weren't perfect. God seriously became the love of my life and the zeal I had to serve Him was so strong.

Yet, though I was forgiven, and I knew that, my past was so fresh. I was a baby Christian. Everything was so recent and happening so fast. I still hadn't gotten over the fact that I had strayed for so long, before returning to God. I grew up in the church, so deep down inside, I knew better.

Now it was my eleventh grade year and the campus ministry I had joined at the end of my tenth grade year, was having an election. I sat there in the classroom, thinking back to where I had come from in the past year, thankful for where God had me at that moment. At some of the previous meetings, I had volunteered to share what was on my heart. That was when I was comfortable, at moments when I was ready to utilize my basic skill of encouragement, to uplift my fellow schoolmates for the day.

This meeting went for a turn. I was nominated, and voted to be the president of my high school Christian club for the rest of the eleventh grade year. Meaning, I would have to compose sermons every month to share with the group, as well as preaching at our school wide events. I didn't mind sharing the gospel, but this felt like being a preacher. At that time, I didn't know the difference.

For a while, I just stepped up to the plate. I wasn't doing anything different than I had been doing. I continued spending time with God. I continued getting into His word. This time, I just shared whatever He had given me, to every one else. Yet, the tests started to come quickly and things became hard.

Preachers have a very big responsibility and will be held at a higher judgment on the very last day. To be a teacher of the gospel, you have to be called. The Bible says in James 3:1 (NLT), "Dear brothers and sisters, not many of you should become teachers in the church, for we who teach will be judged more strictly."

I got involved with a new guy, and started getting distracted from the path God had me on. Soon after this guy and I started dating, we were getting too close physically. I started to feel guilty about what I was doing, and began feeling guilty again, for my past. I knew that I couldn't be a hypocrite, especially now that the students within the organization would often come to me for advice on the issues that they were dealing with in their lives.

Toward the end of the year, I stepped down from my position as the president of the Christian club. I really couldn't bear the responsibility at the place that I was in with my walk with God. The sponsor of the organization was very disappointed, and the Vice President, who had seemingly been looking up to me until then, expressed his disappointment as well. I felt like I failed them, but I'd rather be honest with myself and let them down than be dishonest with everyone else, and let God down.

I decided to spend my senior year at a different school, so all of the responsibility fell back on my Vice President. He ended up going through what I went through the next year. He would contact me often, asking for advice on being a leader, because he was having issues with purity, and preaching the messages. I didn't know. I was traumatized by the experience myself.

During senior year, I had developed my newfound love for spoken word poetry after getting saved. My history teacher that year was very much about teaching us how to be leaders and active citizens within our community. He petitioned that the administrative staff permit him to add a "free speech zone" outside of the cafeteria during lunchtime. He wanted us, his students, to practice our freedom of speech. On that platform, the rule was: we could say whatever we wanted.

Some people sang, some people ranted, and some people shared. I spit poetry. I shared the gospel of truth and I wasn't ashamed about it. I loved that I had the opportunity to speak at my own will rather than feeling forced to do it. The art form of spoken word gave me the ability to share the truth without sounding "preachy" or judgmental to my school full of kids with diverse beliefs. They admired my skill and the way that I strategically used it to get my message across. Though it did not seem like preaching, it was still achieving a similar goal in that moment in time. People were learning about Jesus and what it meant to have a relationship with Him.

My poetry was saturated with Biblical references and testimonies of my own life. I was comfortable because I was not presented under a title. I did not feel the pressure of being the preacher, I felt like myself. I was the imperfect sinner, saved by grace through faith. I was the girl who had her share of unhealthy relationships, the girls who for so long ran after useless idols and put so many other things before God, and I was still able to stand there and share the truth.

Fellow students would come up to me, telling me how they were inspired and/or changed by my poetry. I knew it was not me they were inspired by. It was not about the skill that was given to me. Rather, it was about the message. It was about meeting the need in that place, when no one else was there to do so.

I went to college the next year, and no sooner than that, I was on the executive board for a spoken word organization there. It didn't take long for me to realize that the message I had was very different from a lot of messages that were emerging out of the group. Though I loved my organization members dearly, and made good friends, I eventually stepped down because of my differentiating views with the direction of some of the organizations events.

Still, I attended the events though filled with messages that opposed mine. I only attended so that I could share my poems that shed truth and light in the midst of what I knew was darkness. To my surprise, I was very respected during this time, though many students may have disagreed with what I said, many commentated on how they were inspired by my boldness to stand up for something that many Christians come to college and put in their back pockets.

See, I was not willing to give up on my beliefs because some philosophy teacher on my college campus said Jesus was not God. I knew the truth. I spent so much time in it, college was not the time for me to run away, but face these tests face-front.

Your very life, the decisions you make, the way you live, can be a sermon for someone who never set foot in a church. You can inspire change, by simply being unashamed of what you believe in. One of my favorite poets, Karness Turner, performed an awesome poem a few years ago called, "Does Anyone Know You're a Christian?" This poem definitely had a great impact on me in the beginning of my walk with Christ. It talks about how we are meant to be a light in this world, not to blend in and act as the world acts. Matthew 5:14 (NIV) says, "You are the light of the world. A town built on a hill cannot be hidden." Our college campuses are pervaded with so much unbelief these days. Standing up for God is crucial, especially in a time as this.

One day last semester, outside of the union on my college campus, there was a preacher, with many billboards up, sharing the gospel of Jesus Christ. This was great. He had done this many times, because I had seen him before. This time was a little different though. Across from where he was, there was a false preacher and a mob of unbelievers, blaspheming God and trying to make noise to overpower what this preacher was saying.

At first, I tried to ignore it. A circle of us surrounded the preacher who spoke the truth about the Bible. Some posed the question, "What about people who are born homosexual, why are Christians such homophobes?" I raised my hand. The preacher called on me to speak.

"When I was younger, I thought I was gay. I didn't know who I was and I searched for my identity in relationships. When I accepted Jesus, I found my true identity, in Him. This August, I just married the man of my dreams."

They were astounded.

"I respect that," a lot of them said.

Sometimes, just sharing your testimony, and what Jesus did for you, can be all a person needs to hear in order to change.

Anyway, I didn't want to stay and feel the attention on me so I went on my way to the mob that was across from us. As I got closer, I could hear their foolishness. I tried to flush out all the lies and the deceit that were going forth, and I began to pray. I began to pray silently in tongues, and just in general, asking God to give me strength and have His way. Honestly, I was getting angry, sweaty—I took off my backpack, then my jacket, and put them down on the nearest picnic bench to me. I was pacing back and forth. A righteous anger sprung up in me. I felt the strong urge to say something, the need to defend my Savior, their Savior, too. I looked into the crowd and spotted a few believers I knew. *Why were they just blending in? How can they watch this and not say anything?*

The false preacher was standing on at the cement edge of a raised garden. Suddenly, I stepped open the platform. I spit, at the highest and most clear volume that my mouth would let out. He laughed at me, pointed fingers, and made blasphemous comments, trying to get me off track, trying to get me to forget my words and stumble. Glory be to God, my eyes went past him like x-ray vision. Not one word was lost. I was so focused in on the message; nothing was going to get me off track. More and more, the crowd grew silent. The eyes of many, believers and non-believers, locked in with mine one by one. It's like they were waiting to be reminded that they had a decision to make. They wanted to know that there was another way.

I was the light God turned on. I was the light on the hill... but it could have been anyone of them. It could be you. When I was done, I stepped down and grabbed my things. People came up to me and said "That was brave", "I respect that", ... and sometimes I wish they knew, that it was more—more than me.

Spiritual Insight on How to Share the Gospel:

The best way to share the gospel without becoming a traditional preacher is by simply spreading the truth in love. We can share the gospel by living it out in our day-to-day lives and showing the world what the true love of Christ looks like. This is an area that we should constantly be looking to grow in—love. As it says in I Corinthians 13:2, "If I have the gift of prophecy and can fathom all mysteries and all knowledge, and if I have faith that can move mountains, but do not have love, I am nothing." If we lived our lives as fervent lovers of God, while showing true love toward others, our lives would preach themselves and people would want to know about this God we serve, especially if we have determined to do so at such a young age.

Practical Insight on How to Share the Gospel:

1. Share your testimony every opportunity you get!

I share my testimony all the time! In school, I was a creative writing major and wrote a lot of essays and many of them had a pretty open ended prompt. I took advantage of open ended writing prompts because I used them as opportunities to share my testimony and talk about Jesus. The best thing about these writing classes is that we had workshops where other students in the class were required to read our papers very closely and critically. Because of that, I had chances to share my testimony with classmates who were fornicating, addicted to alcohol, depressed, etc. At first, you may think that non-believers will read your paper and tear it to shreds! That's what I thought, but God was pushing me to take that big leap of faith, and it turns out… even though the majority of the people in my classes weren't Christian, they were very respectful toward my views and inspired by my testimony. Sometimes, they even asked if I could share my final draft or portfolio with them at the end of the semester!

Another way to share your faith is during class discussion! I was never afraid to say the name of Jesus in class! I am not afraid to share my views but be ready for backlash during class discussion. You better know your word and know what you're talking about! Class discussion can be an awesome tool because *every single person* in that class is listening and watching you… even the one's who sit in the back and never say anything.

2. Don't go with the crowd!

Just because they're going to the club doesn't mean you have to go! Just because the crowd is against Jesus doesn't mean you have to sit back and blend in, either!

3. Answer questions about your faith in boldness.

Do not back down. In class, your professor might make comments like, "All of you guys go to the club right? You're college students…" Don't be afraid to say, "Well I don't". It's okay to be the only one to raise your hand on the opposing side when a yes or no question is asked relating to your faith. Raise it proudly! I would raise my hand high and proud! I always vote in class because a non-voter is generally a lukewarm person who's afraid someone will judge them.

4. Don't worry about being "cool".

You can't afford cool.

Gospel Sharing Resources:

- **Bible:** The most important resource you'll ever need in life is the Bible. I like different versions for different reasons. Get a version that you can understand.

  - **Kings James Version:** Because first translation of the Bible, therefore, it's closest to the original.

  - **New Kings James Version:** Because it's a more understandable version of Kings James.

  - **The Amplified Bible:** The work of breaking down scripture is done for you. It's rather an exhaustive and expansive look at scripture. Still, sometimes you want to do the work by yourself because you can learn from the process of breaking down scripture.

- Some bibles have really good features that could help you in your study. Some of these *features* include but are not limited to:
  - Maps of Jerusalem, and other locations mentioned in the Bible
  - Devotionals
  - Topic organization
  - Notes

- Historical accounts and context of Bible text

- Historical accounts of persons in the Bible

- Concordance

- **Audio Bible:** Great to play at nights when sleeping, or when you have your fingers tied washing the dishes, or folding laundry. Even if we're not 100% alert, having the word of God in our subconscious can definitely make a difference and help us remember scripture.

  - The Bible App in the App Store gives the option of playing in audio.

- **Concordance:** I like Bibles that have concordances, but this can always be bought or used separately. In a Bible concordance, you will be able to locate where specific words are used in different parts of the Bible. This is a great tool because it helps in correlating scripture "in accordance" with other scripture and passages in the Bible.

  - A good handheld concordance:

    - Strong's Exhaustive Concordance

    - This could also be found online at several sites:

      - www.biblestudytools.com

      - www.biblegateway.com

      - www.biblehub.com

- **Greek and Hebrew Dictionaries:**

  - The Bible was original written in Hebrew (Old Testament) and Greek (New Testament). A lot of times, the true meanings of words can become lost in the English translation. Using Greek and Hebrew dictionaries, which can also be found online in the above sites, or simply doing an online search for words in Greek and Hebrew, can help you get to the original meanings of many of the words written in the Bible.

- **Biblical Commentaries:**

  - Biblical commentaries are not so often used but can be helpful when considering the different possibilities of interpretation of a certain passage of scripture, as well as witnessing someone else's revelation and insight. Though these are great, the Holy Spirit does a great job of leading, opening our eyes, and providing His own biblical commentary on a day-to-day basis.

Young Missionary Shares the Gospel of Love

Damaris Payen | 21 yrs. young, *Miami, Florida*

My desire is to help the lost, the hurting, the broken, and the needy discover their identity in Christ and become true Disciples of Christ. My vision, as Matthew 28:19-20 sums up, is to go out into the world and make Disciples, teach them, and have them go and make Disciples of Christ. The Lord allows me to be the voice of these people when no one else will hear them. I no longer use my outspokenness to be detrimental to my life but solely to glorify the Lord and love His people.

I am fully aware of all the resources, knowledge, and support I will need to fulfill the calling the Lord has placed over my life at such a young age. It wasn't until I found the Lord at the age of 14 that I discovered why He placed my aunts as living examples for me to watch when I was a little girl and allowed me to triumph over every circumstance I encountered in my childhood and adolescent years. By pursuing my passion, I will be able to open up homes and centers dedicated to coaching, counseling, teaching, reintegrating, and liberating each individual to walk in the fullness of their God-given calling. Currently, I am counseling people (friends, family, and strangers). I lead a women's Bible study called "Pillars of Grace" with my sister; some friends, family, and I have started a movement called "Touch of Healing- South Florida", which is geared to helping those in need of any kind in the South Florida area. This will soon become a non-profit organization and eventually grow to be group homes, philanthropies, and shelters. I am working my way into becoming a Caribbean missionary, providing whatever necessities these countries may be lacking (I went on my first mission trip to Nicaragua for 2 weeks in July of 2013). I was able to raise money to send two medical students in Nicaragua back to Medical school, raised over $500 for a homeless man to buy a new car, and I am working to ship about 30 Bibles over to Nicaragua to assist in the spiritual growth of the youth in Little Corn Island, Nicaragua. I am currently completing my nursing degree and a degree in counseling so that I may be able to do medical missions and open up centers to help people discover their God-given purpose worldwide.

I refuse to give up on people when God never gave up on me and I know that the Holy Spirit will teach me everything I need to know to become a Christ-centered leader for God and a light to His people. There is so much God has purposed in my heart that I refuse to allow go to the grave with me. As Jesus said a minute before He died, "It is finished". All this and I'm only 21 years old. As the saying goes, "If I can do it, so can you."

YOU CAN **PUBLISH A BOOK**

Publishing a book is not the same as it was in the past. With fewer barriers, time restraints, and a new emergence of the self-publishing industry, new authors are rising up left to right. If you wanted to publish a book in the past, you most likely had to go through a publishing company and work years at getting your manuscript approved and perfected the way they want it. The good news is that, today, there are so many different resources and routes available for you to publish your own book. The good thing about this is: you get to control the entire process. If you really want to publish your book, regardless of your age, experience, or skill, you can.

My beginnings as a writer may have not been the best. But when I tell you that God can take weaknesses and turn them into strengths, believe me, He can. At the beginning of my primary school years, I could remember struggling with things as simple as writing my name. I remember sitting in my Grandma's home office for hours, just practicing to get *Karolyne* written in the right way.

School was a struggle for me, I barely made it by with my grades, but after encountering a life transition and moving away from South Florida to the little town of Broken Arrow in Oklahoma, my education was in for a turn. The year I moved, I was entering the third grade. I was living with my aunt, who had once lived across the street from us in Miramar, Florida.

Now, living there under my aunts roof was, of course, different than just going over there to play every once in a while like I used to. My aunt was now the official boss over me because my mother was thousands of miles away, and I didn't know it then, but that year would change my life forever.

My aunt was very much involved with the academics of everyone who lived under her roof. Therefore, it didn't take her long to realize that I was having some struggles with school. She took immediate action, and signed me up for a tutoring program that I went to every day after school. My tutor helped me with math, reading, spelling, and so on.

After my first day of tutoring, I got home and after completing my homework, my aunt said, "Go read a book". I said, "I don't have a book." and shocked her pants off. She told me to go to my school library the next day and said that I better not come back to her house again if I don't have some books. My third grade self took this as a very serious threat, so the next day, I was sure to go to the library.

I librarian recommended that I read Junie B. Jones, *First Grader*. I loved Junie B. Jones' books. Later, I had grown obsessed with Harry Potter and read it in secret because my aunt was devout a Christian woman, and didn't agree with the witchcraft presented in those novels. Even though I would never let my own kids read Harry Potter now, I will say that those thick books really taught me how to read!

After I would get home from tutoring every day, Tati Florence, my aunt, would have me read at least a chapter in a book and answer her questions about what I read. If she couldn't do it one day, she'd ask my uncle to do it, but she did it, every single day. She made it very clear that school days were school days, no TV was allowed until our homework was finished, reading was finished, and we finished off our dinner. Usually by that time, it was bedtime.

It worked. I went into the third grade scoring well bellow my grade average. By the grace of God, I continued to increase my vocabulary and reading comprehension until I was scoring in middle school level on my reading placement tests toward the end of my third grade year.

In those moments when I was struggling in school, I did not know that I would end up being a poet, and author of two books at the mere age of 21 years. God is amazing! The first book I wrote, *Before Saying 'Yes' to the Ring*, received a response that I really did not expect. Still, when writing the book, I had prayed earnestly to God that He would use my book and I to impact the lives of our younger generation. I was blown away after receiving 5 star ratings and messages from people in the US, UK, and Africa, saying how my book had impacted their life.

The amazing part of it all is that I was able to self-publish my book, with the help of the Holy Spirit. After doing that, I became passionate about helping other people get their book projects off the ground. I want people to experience the fulfillment that I have experienced throughout this journey, and do what God has called them to do!

For that reason, my husband and I started our own publishing company, IAMIMAGE Publishing, where we combine editing skills and our graphic and web design skills to help publish and market people's books. My husband graduated with a Bachelor of Arts Degree in Graphic Design, and when I met him, he taught me.

It is amazing how God put us together; it is as if He planned our journey all along. He brought us together while having a purpose and vision in mind for us.

My husband was able to leave corporate America within six months of our marriage, even though I was still in college, and since then, we have been living in faith and running our business from home. God has been so faithful, and every month, it has been getting better and better. It is a blessing to be able to say that I have been able to solely focus on my business and the plans God has given me during my college years instead of being pushed and pulled with the distractions of college life.

If God called you to do something, don't be afraid. The Holy Spirit taught me everything I know, and has been with me every step of the way. Has God laid a message on your heart that He has been leading you to share with the masses? Answer the call. Don't let your age or the thought of your weaknesses keep you being obedient. Don't let your disobedience keep someone else out of heaven. Be willing to share your testimony, be willing to share the gospel. Don't underestimate the power that God can use to work through you. He will put the very words you need to write, on that paper!

Spiritual Insight on How to Publish a Book:

- Pray for your book before you write and when you're writing it. Before you write, pray to God that you say everything He wants you to say. Nothing more, and nothing less. Pray that the Holy Spirit writes through you. Pray for your desired goal. Do you desire that people will be changed? Informed? Saved? Or that your book will spread across the nations? Whatever it is, pray for it. I make prayer for my book and the people who will read it a natural habit. Trust me, it works!

- Don't be afraid to fast when writing your book. If you have a very specific goal to break spiritual chains and strongholds off of the lives of your readers, fasting would be a very good way to go about it, as well as a good way the clearly hear what the Lord is telling you to write. A fast means sacrificing something from your life for a time, and replacing that sacrifice with prayer and spending time with God, knowing that He is the one who fills any voids and makes us whole. Some people fast from food, from communication, etc. In writing this book, I fasted from social media and I was able to hear God clearer. I also wrote a major portion of this book during that time and prayed. Before fasting, pray to God for His will and if it's a physical fast having to do with sacrificing food etc., consult your doctor first, in case of health issues.

- Don't be afraid to go deeper if you're using Bible verses or passages of scripture in your book. Don't just take this as a time to preach to others, but as a time to really learn from the Holy Spirit. Everything you research may not be shared in your book. But, the research will help you develop your knowledge of the topic and it will definitely impact your confidence and affect your writing in the way you address the topic. Also, if questioned about certain parts of your book later, you'll be able to backup what you wrote by sharing what you studied.

Practical Insight on How to Publish a Book:

- Write an outline of what you want to talk about. That way, you're able to organize your thoughts, while, at the same time, making a list so that you don't skip over anything. Writing an outline will also help with the flow of the book and help create structure so that others will better comprehend the message you are trying to send.

- Write, write, write, and don't stop or hold back! Write until you can't write anymore, meaning that you've gotten your point across and there's nothing purposeful left to write about... don't focus on the mechanics when you're writing because it will slow down your process. At the end, you'll be able to go back, take out what you don't want to be there, put back in what you missed or realized, and clean up the mess.

- Ask yourself a lot of questions and answer them. You want to know what you're writing and what message you want to get across because when you publish your book, others will be asking you the questions you should know. Being an authority on what you're saying and being knowledgeable is what will cause others to buy your book and take you seriously. Ask yourself questions like: What inspired me to write this book? Do I expect to gain anything out of this, if so, then what? Who am I writing to? Do I have a target audience? Can I back up what I'm saying?

- Clear your mind before you write. You want your thoughts to be clear on the page, and not jumbled. You also want your words to be true and not influenced by negative emotions. Find what time or place works best for your writing. Some people find that going near a lake to write is where their mind is most clear and they're most inspired to write. For others, it's right in their closet where they have prayer time in the middle of the night. Find what place and time works for you.

- Market your book ahead of time, meaning, let people know it's coming out a while before. Get people excited and have them anticipate the coming of your book. If possible, accept opportunities to speak to the media and press about the book and why it was so important for you to write. (God-willing)

- Gather your resources by finding a publishing company that will publish your book, or if you're self publishing, look into publishing consultants or individual professionals who will help in the production of your book such as graphic designers for the cover, editors for the manuscript, and/or illustrators if you are looking to write a children's book.

- Involve family and friends by having them donate to your publishing expenses or throwing a book signing/launch party so they can support you and spread the word. Or if that's not God's will, trust Him to fund it for you 100%!

Book Publishing Resources:

- **IAMIMAGE.com:** Our publishing company can help you write, publish, design, and market your book.

- **Self-publishing Websites:**
    - www.Createspace.com
    - Blurb.com
    - Lulu.com

- **Kdp.Amazon.com:** Publish your eBook online.

- **Www.bookmarket.com/publishing.htm:** Has a lot of detailed information on book publishing resources.

Young Pastor Writes a Bestseller!

Jamal Miller | 24 yrs. young, Chicago, Illinois

It was at the age of 12 years old that I was first told I would not only write one book, but multiple books. Hearing those words made my spirit leap because it was a destiny that one day I would soon walk in. When in college, I had many book ideas, and even went as far as creating an outline for some. But, something would happen, and I would leave the project to the wayside. It wasn't until my wife and I started a movement called Married and Young, which began as a blog, but now has become a full force brand and resource for young marriages. The amount of people we came into relation with desired more than an article from me. They put a demand on the very thing I continually put on the shelf. I still had no idea what I would do a book on, until I wrote an article called, "25 Ways to Prepare for Marriage Other than Dating". This article was the starting point for my first book that would later become a #1 Hot New Release on Amazon within 12 hours of launching. I'm going to briefly give you 4 steps to successfully publishing your first book in 90 days.

1. Embrace the God of _____ (7 Days)

    • You can find the phrase repeatedly throughout the Old Testament, "We serve the God of Abraham, Isaac, and Jacob." I remember the first time God whispered that to me. "Many will come behind you and say, "We worship the God of Jamal Miller". It sounded weird, but it was true. Many will benefit from my history and experience with God. It is out of your life that your book will carry your DNA. No one has your experience and story that will make that topic come alive with your fingerprint. So, be you. Write your book like no one else can. What God has done in you, and through you, has the power to encourage the masses, but it won't until you first embrace the God of _____(fill in your name)

2. Just do it. (40 days)

- Now, once you embrace your story and get a concept for what you want to write on, it is very key to have a headline that draws, which we will cover better in the next step. With your content, do not hold back. Just do it! I gave myself a 500 word a day goal, which is the length of an average blog article. I wouldn't go to sleep at night unless I had written my 500 words. In 40 days, you will have 20,000 words completed, which is a 100 page paperback book! Now, you can set your own pace, but I wanted to show you what I was able to do with determination.

3. Get Your World's Attention. (40 Days)

- After you have your major content, you need to get the World's attention. First, find an editor who can edit your book, and while that phase is in action, you can move toward marketing. Determine who the book will benefit most, and do everything to draw that audience. Your book cover design will make or break your book. I had our M&Y audience help choose from 2 different designs. This was a marketing strategy to get them involved in the process. I also sent my finished manuscript to a group of 50 people for free, with the agreement for them to share it on their social media platforms and to write a review on Amazon. Your book will only goes as far as you plan for it to go. Research marketing strategies for self-publishers and find strategies that work for you and your targeted audience. If it changes their life, then they will share it because that's just human nature.

4. Enjoy the reward.

- Enjoy what God has done yet again in your life. Many will thank you for putting in the time to write such a wonderful work, but remember: it's just the beginning. Writing a book is two fold. It blesses others, and it will bless you.

YOU CAN **BE A ROLE MODEL**

When people think of a role model, they think of someone who has "made it". They may look up to someone who has financial freedom, quality relationships, and happiness. What I have come to realize is that role models can be in different places in life. In our society, a role model has become the generalized figure and picture of success. The truth is, we are all different, so a role model will be different for each person, and will most likely have a relatable aspect to that of the admirer. People who are even older than me have come to me for advice and said that they look up to me. It baffles me, until I remember that it's not me, it's the God living inside of me, who I model myself after.

Our distinctions don't only lie in age. Our distinctions lie in the different places we are in life, in mind, and in spirit. For that reason, you can have multiple role models. You can admire someone who has a positive mindset and admire someone else who has a healthy spiritual walk with God. Believe it or not, these can be two completely different types of people, in different places in life, or, they can be the same person. I may be a role model for some people because of my business personality, and to others, it may be because of my love for God. Whatever it is, a role model is not about being on top of the world in every aspect. A role model is one who is relatable to others, and inspires them to strive or become of something that is actually attainable.

When I was younger, I used to look up to people who I thought, "looked good" (on the outside). My idea of success was beauty and money. If you had that, you were a "boss". If you had that, you were "independent". You were the type of person I looked up to.

At that point in my life, which was around my late middle school years, I was so shallow and I strived to dedicate my life to looking good on the outside, having the hottest clothes, friends, and boyfriends so I could be noticed by my peers.

That mindset brought so much drama to my life. It lead me to unhealthy and superficial relationships. Lastly, no one else was looking up to me for how I was acting. I wasn't setting a good example for my little sister, or anyone else for that matter.

I went through a phase where I wanted to be a model so bad. *America's Next Top Model* was my favorite show. It was basically an idol to me, something that I worshiped and looked up to more than God. I watched it over and over, re-run after re-run, and my life's goal was to one day be old enough to audition for *America's Next Top Model*. In the meantime, I went to casting calls and joined modeling agencies, etc. All those things wasted my money, for what I thought I wanted to be.

I didn't want to be a fashion model. Deep down inside, I knew that I wanted to be someone who people looked up to, but I didn't have a clear understanding of what that meant; for me that meant everything carnal rather than spiritual.

I understand now that this limited mindset was simply because I didn't have a relationship Christ. Therefore, I didn't have a spiritual perspective. My mind was strictly worldly. In high school, when I finally began to develop a relationship with God after getting out of a verbally abusive and sinful relationship, I gained a better perspective of the type of model I wanted to be. I wanted to be like Jesus.

I didn't want to be a fashion model or a video vixen. I wanted to be a role model. I wanted to be someone other young adults can look up to, be inspired by, and pushed to have a better life and a relationship with God. Shortly after I truly was saved, in 2010, I wrote a declaration of the type of woman I wanted to be. To this day, five years later, I still have that declaration, and I want to share it with you:

I want to be modest but beautiful. I want to be me. I want to be and feel so beautiful that I know and everyone else knows that it's not my clothes, hair, nails, and those things that make me beautiful. I want to give, love others, and change lives. I don't want to be judgmental. I want to be loving, but I know I can't love and draw people until I love myself. I want to carry myself so well. I want to eat right, dress uniquely but modestly, keep a healthy and fit body, and take care of my body. I want to be an achiever. I want to set goals and accomplish every one of them, God willing. I want to stop procrastinating and start working hard for my success. I want to be responsible in the way I manage my time. I want to always put God first. I want to focus on a few things at a time so I could do a very good job at them. I want to use my other time to get closer to God and gain guidance to keep moving forward. I want to explore the artistic gifts that God has given me and master them. I want to apply all those gifts to His Kingdom. I want to be financially prosperous and faithful in tithing, offering, and sowing seeds. I want to be so financially prosperous that I reach a point where I can constantly bless others and not have to worry about my financial stability. I want to have such a strong faith that my faith becomes reality. I want my intercession to change lives and I want my faith to make my dreams come true. I want to have authority over all of the yokes that the Lord has broken off of my life and over all sin. I want to live in the fullness of the blessing. I want God to use me. I want to do God's will 2010/2011.

At the time that I wrote this, I was nowhere near where I hoped to be. Looking at where I am now, I can say that I am amazed at how God took that note, that declaration, and showed me that He answers prayers. Little by little throughout the years, I've found myself checking off certain parts of my letter, because I finally began to see the fruit of who I wanted to be. To this day, there are still many things that haven't been perfected in me, or haven't come into fruition yet, but I am honored to see how far God has chosen to take me.

I eventually gave up on the modeling, and started finding myself behind the camera. In 2010, I discovered my love for photography. There was something special about taking the focus off of me and how I looked, and directing that energy to uplifting someone else's self-image. This was around the same time that I began to write and perform poetry; I was finding every way to uplift others. For the first time ever, I realized that life wasn't all about me, and there was a bigger purpose out there. There were people out there, just like me, who needed God, who had broken relationships, unhealthy mindsets, and false doctrines. There is no time to be consumed with me! Being a model is all about you; being a role model, is about everyone else.

I joined groups of friends to do photography events for charity and orphanages in Haiti. To me, photography was never about money. Though my business also provides photography services, the living I make out of it does not come from the money. The living I'm talking about is the lifestyle and experiences that come out of having the opportunity to minister to others about their true worth and identity, uplift them, and through Christ, rid them of any ounce of low self-esteem. Ultimately, a role model is not consumed with receiving attention from others; rather, directing any attention they receive, back to the God who lives inside of them.

Spiritual Insight on How to Be a Role Model

So then how can you be a role model for others? Well, firstly, you have to focus on developing you. A lot of people are ready to tell people what they should do, and how they should live, but they haven't even shown consistent fruit of what they are saying.

Showing fruit means having proof in your life of the good things going on inside of you. Therefore, you start by planting seeds within you that will grow to bear beautiful fruit. The seeds that I am talking about, of course, aren't natural seeds, but spiritual seeds.

Your heart is the soil that grows these seeds, so you need to make sure that your heart is in the proper condition to bear the best fruit possible. You heart needs to be pure, and full of nutrients and good things, just like good soil.

In Mark 4, there is a parable about a seed sower. Seeds were sown on three different grounds. Some are sown by the way side, some on stony ground, and some on good ground. Those grounds are reflections of our hearts. Is your heart like the wayside? Meaning, are you a wayward and lukewarm Christian? Do you have one foot inside of the world and another foot out?

The Bible says, "And it came to pass, as he sowed, some fell by the way side, and the fowls of the air came and devoured it up." (Mark 4:4) Those are the type of people who think that they can live both ways, but it's easier to walk down a hill than up a hill. Being in the world will open you up so fowls of the air can come in and snatch the seeds that have been sown in your heart, taking them away from you. Meaning that you will never have the opportunity to grow or bear actual fruit.

Is your heart like the stony ground? Has it been so hardened toward God that you refuse to let anything grow? Soil has to be soft. Meaning that for you to bear fruit, you need to let God's love penetrate your heart. You need to let forgiveness find its way to your soil, more specifically, your soul. Mark 4:5-6 says, "And some fell on stony ground, where it had not much earth; and immediately it sprang up, because it had no depth of earth: But when the sun was up, it was scorched; and because it had no root, it withered away." When you have darkness in your heart, you have no depth. Imagine a pitch-black room. When everything is black, nothing looks close or far away. Everything is one dimensional, black, right before your face. Without any depth, you won't be able to have firm roots and stand upon God's truth.

Imagine now, having a room with some light. Light that came from love, forgiveness, and a hope to change. Some areas will be highlighted very brightly and some areas will have shadows... but the lighting creates a depth and a three dimensionality that darkness alone can never create. When the sun comes up, instead of scorching the plants you have grown, being that black attracts much heat, the amount of sun will be healthy enough to grow the seeds. Everyone knows that with planting, you need some type of sun. Furthermore, your plants need to be in the right position, so that the sun can be of use. In the same way, your heart needs to be soft, have some depth, and be in good enough condition, so that the word of God can effectively grow its seeds that have been planted within you.

Do you have a thorny heart? Do you hate God, and look for arguments about the Bible so that you can battle it every chance you get? If you keep doing this, you will never bear fruit. You will prick out everything good from growing in your heart because you refuse to accept that there is a true God, and that His word is the final say. According to Mark 4:7, "And some fell among thorns, and the thorns grew up, and choked it, and it yielded no fruit."

Or does the good ground represent your heart? Have you softened any soil that was once hard or uprooted any thorns? Have you decided to fully surrender your entire life and self to God? Then you have good soil. The Bible says, "And other fell on good ground, and did yield fruit that sprang up and increased; and brought forth, some thirty, and some sixty, and some a hundred" (Mark 4:8). Now having fruit like this, with thirty, sixty, and a hundred fold, that is what makes you a role model.

People never want to hear how to live, especially if they're already dealing with the wrong soil. They want to see it. Show them that this Christian life your living isn't just a fad… it's an actual lifestyle. Show them that it's possible because it is. You can be young and serve God. At the moment, I am 21 years old. Instead of spending these years drinking, partying, or having sex, I am married to the love of my life, Jesus Christ. I am married to my natural husband, on this earth, and helping people build their businesses and the visions God has given them every day. God is just looking for some good soil to plant His seed. He is looking for a pure and willing heart.

Practical Insight on How to Be a Role Model

- **It starts at home:** You're willing to be a parent to everyone else, except your own child. You're willing to serve every other ministry, except for your church at home. This should not be. Be faithful with little, and God will trust you with more.

- **Start a blog:** Share your journey as you're going through it. You can connect with people all across the world that need to hear of your example.

- **Don't be afraid:** Set the standard. Do the thing that most people wouldn't. Obey God and step outside of your comfort zone.

- **Be yourself:** To be a role model, you need to embrace your individuality. Being unique is the best example you can set for someone looking up to you. You want to spread this message, so that others won't follow you and try to be like you, but that they will be inspired by you to find themselves in Christ.

Role Model Resources:

- **YouTube Search:**
    - Inspirational Speakers: It's good to listen to people's stories. You may be able to relate with where they came from.
    - How to start a blog

- **Blog Websites** (Create free blogs using these sites):
    - Blogger.com
    - Wordpress.com
    - Wix.com

- **Find cool blog templates/themes:**
    - Themeforest.com
    - Elegantthemes.com

- **Boys and Girls Club America:** Community service mentorship program
    - Bgcbb.com

Young Dancer Models Her Life After Christ!

Cierra Cotton | 25 yrs. old, Atlanta, Georgia

"Young people, it's wonderful to be young! Enjoy every minute of it. Do everything you want to do; take it all in. But remember that you must give an account to God for everything you do..."Don't let the excitement of youth cause you to forget to honor your Creator. Honor Him in your youth before you grow old..." Ecclesiastes 11:9, 12:1

As a 25-year-old female who is living for the Lord, I fully recognize that the lifestyle I lead is far from ordinary. While I'm chasing hard after Christ, most of my peers are chasing after money, guys/girls, fame, pleasure, and other temporal things that have no eternal value. On a Saturday night, when most people are getting ready to party and "turn up", you can find me and my girlfriends having a girls night in, watching movies, talking about God and what He's teaching us, sharing words of encouragement, and cooking for one another. I actually have so much more fun now than I ever did when I was attempting to party the world's way, plus I get more sleep!

I grew up in the church and at a young age came to know the Lord. I wish I could say that I stayed focused and never strayed from Him but that's definitely not the case. Like a lot of people, around my teenage years, I fell away and started to live to please my own selfish desires. Instead of turning to the Lord to help direct my every step, I took matters into my own hands. As a result, I became super insecure and lonely, my self-esteem was non-existent, I got my heart broken multiple times, I fell in and out of depression, was filled with jealousy, and developed a crazy judgmental and critical mindset. At the time, I didn't realize just how broken I was on the inside.

Throughout high school and most of college, I failed countless times at trying to fill the growing void in my heart with everyone and everything, except the one person who was capable of making me whole and complete, Jesus Christ. I had lost all sense of self-worth and placed my identity in temporal things of the world instead of in Christ.

Once I turned 21, I sought to try to escape my problems by drinking and occasionally going out with friends to clubs and lounges. I spent so much time and energy trying to "fit in" with the world but I never found the satisfaction or acceptance I was searching for. I was straddling the fence, trying to live halfway in the world and halfway in the Kingdom, and it was super exhausting. The Holy Spirit was constantly convicting me and I was tired of feeling guilty and ashamed of the decisions I was making. Eventually, I had enough and just cried out to God, asking Him to help me. I was done trying to lead my life and was ready to submit to His plan and will for my life.

At the time, I was living in New York City, working as a freelance professional dancer and teaching dance to children. I loved what I was doing but the more I sought God and submitted unto Him, the more I felt like I wasn't supposed to be there anymore. The little bit of peace I did have about living in NYC was quickly fading away. One fall morning, when I was sitting outside having quiet time and writing in my journal, the Lord spoke to me saying that I would be moving from NYC in the near future, that He was calling me to go elsewhere soon. I had no idea when, where, or for what purpose, but God promised to see me through it all.

About three months later, in December of 2012, after diligently praying and fasting, the Lord finally revealed to me that He wanted me to move to Atlanta and attend the Gathering Oasis Church that Cornelius and Heather Lindsey were starting that following month. I didn't fully understand why but after spending so many years doing my own thing, I was more than ready to try something different. I prayed that God would give me the desire to step out on faith and not live by sight anymore, that I would live outside of my comfort zone and take the necessary risks to experience all that He had planned for my life. Immediately, my mind began to be attacked by the enemy and doubt and fear started to creep into my heart but God continued to confirm over and over what He told me and I began to make preparations to move to Atlanta.

Fast forward to May and there I was packing up to leave New York City. I didn't have a car or job but felt God really pushing me to leave. He started closing doors of opportunity and breaking ties with the people who I had become close with over the past six years. My parents came and got me from NYC and I spent a week in Baltimore but the entire time, I knew in my heart that God wanted me in Atlanta. Baltimore was a just pit stop and an opportunity to rest before the journey ahead. I spent a lot of the week in prayer and finally, I woke up that Friday and said, "Lord, if it is in your will for me to move to Atlanta, please help me to find a safe and reliable car in my price range today." Guess what happened four hours later? I had a car with tags, title, and insurance. The best part was that I was able to pay for it in cash. Three days later, I stepped out on faith, packed my car up, and made the drive down to Atlanta from Baltimore without any idea of what to expect. I just prayed that the Lord would continue to guide my steps.

From the moment I arrived in Atlanta, God began to open doors for me. At times, I doubted Him, faced crazy attacks from the enemy, and almost gave up and moved back to Baltimore but He was faithful and kept me through it all, which helped me learn to truly rely on Him. God has challenged me to grow and changed my desires in so many areas. By submitting to His plans and will, He has been able to show me strengths, gifts, talents, and passions I didn't even know I had. One of these passions is my desire to see women in the body of Christ unified, growing in their walk with the Lord, and finding the accountability they need to continue on the race God has set before them.

When I first attended the Gathering Oasis Church, I didn't feel a sense of unity within those who attended. At the time, it was mostly women and there was no fellowship occurring or true relationships being built. We only really spoke to each other on Sundays. God began to place it on my heart to start to plan events for the women and come up with creative ways for us to stay in contact throughout the week. I didn't really think much of it, I just wanted people to get to know one another and really be able to encourage and pray for each other. After a few months of planning events, my pastor approached me and asked if I would be interested in starting up a women's ministry. I was immediately hesitant because I'm more of a behind the scenes type person. I love helping and serving others but the moment you put me in the spotlight, I panic.

The Lord kept leading me to study the story of Moses in Exodus 3 and telling me that He would be with me. He literally began to instruct me in the way to go and gave me the blueprint for what the ministry would be comprised of and how to orchestrate it. The more I studied that text, the more confident I became in wanting to step out and be obedient to the new direction that God was taking my life. It's amazing how He's been more than faithful to provide me with a team of women who have my back, who support and encourage me when things become overwhelming or rough. I've found a new love for praying and interceding on the behalf of others and loving others like Christ loves me.

If you told me a year ago that I would be leading a women's ministry, I wouldn't have believed you. I wouldn't have felt qualified for such a responsibility. If I'm totally honest, there are still times that I feel unqualified to have that position of leadership at such a young age. I would be much more comfortable just helping out in the background and I have to constantly remind myself that God qualifies who He calls.

It's not about how young or old you are, it's about being obedient to God and allowing His glory and light to shine through you. God has called us to be the salt and light of the earth, to be bold and courageous, and to walk by faith and not by sight. Christ didn't die on the cross for us to sit back and be spectators. We are called to be both present and active in whatever the Lord has for us to accomplish.

Looking back over the past 9 months that I've been over the women's ministry at my church, I'm super glad that I was obedient. I get to love on, serve, help, and minister to so many women and put their needs above my own. I'm also learning how to truly lean on the Lord to sustain me and as a result, my relationship with Him is growing stronger each and every day. I absolutely love this season I'm in, despite the tests and trials I have to face because I know without a doubt that I'm walking in God's will for my life.

YOU CAN **BE A LEADER**

During my freshman year of college, I started to go astray. Like a majority of the students, I wanted to try new things and see what that college life was really all about. Trust me, it wasn't about much. It was school and partying, you choose what you want to focus on. When I came in, I was focused on both, but the partying soon brought its distractions along with it.

When I first met my husband during that time, it was in a poetry lounge and I had asked him for a free drink. At the end of the night, he came to me and asked me for my number. Shortly after that, we got caught up with him coming over to my apartment and spending the night. Though I was still a virgin and we didn't have sex, we were still "playing house" and conducting ourselves in a way that was not pleasing to God. We put ourselves in so many tempting situations that we should have never been in.

Eventually God led me to Heather Lindsey's blog, and I can honestly say, Heather was the first true role model I ever had. I read her testimony about how she and her husband waited until their wedding day to kiss. Never in my life had I heard of such thing! Heather wrote a lot on her blog about purity, self-respect, and self-worth. I don't know why this never clicked with me, but seeing someone for the first time, living this way, inspired me to change my ways.

Shortly after being introduced to Heather's blog, I set standards for myself and I also set boundaries between Chris and I. At the time, we were unequally yoked, meaning, we weren't at the same place spiritually. He didn't understand this sudden change or what it meant. We eventually had to break up and take time apart before God brought us back together, changed and transformed. Then we got married.

During our break up, the Lord utilized Heather's organization, Pinky Promise, where the mission is, "A vow to honor God with your life and with your body," as a way to keep me accountable and occupied. I also grew a lot during this time, thanks to Heather's teaching. A true leader is someone who inspires you to change your entire life for the better. It' not just someone who is tells you what to do, but has been there and done that themselves.

I've been able to grow and have many leadership experiences over the past couple of years, but the most influential experience has been with Pinky Promise. When my friend and I first began the organization in our community, we were stunned by the response we received. So many people showed up to our initial meetings, and I knew that I was definitely part of a favored organization, a larger vision.

As months passed though, I came to realize many of my weaknesses as a leader. Some were a lack of communication, a lack of trust toward those who were helping me, and I wasn't truly following up with the girls who had come to our meetings. Eventually, after the organization ended up taking a hiatus, I had to get my heart together concerning leadership, I had to ask the Lord to show me how to lead better, and I also ended up taking a leadership class on my college campus that ended up helping me through this process.

I ended up learning that being a leader wasn't about me, but about everyone else who I was building up to be leaders themselves… it was about the team. Whatever I did needed to be for the betterment of the team, not for my own personal gain, and not to keep me in control or power. Leaders are not afraid of a loss of control. They have enough security and confidence in their goal and purpose for leading, they are able to give away control to others, and empower others to act.

True leaders know that they would be nothing without the team helping them toward achieving a shared goal. Therefore, although discerning, leaders are open to suggestions and commentary, for the well being of the team as a whole, and reaching the desired goal. A leader is not consumed with rank or status to the point where they fear someone else taking over. A leader is focused on the task at hand, and makes sure everyone on the team is equipped and has what they need to reach their greatest potential.

When I came back and started to employ this new mindset, not only did I get more involvement from the girls, but things also began to run more smoothly. I was happy to see a lot of the girls step up and plan community service projects, socials, and other events when I really didn't have the same amount of time to. When I got married, I had to really trust others to act on behalf of the organization, because I had the priority and responsibilities of my home to attend to. I learned the importance of giving others a chance to grow, and making sure everyone is playing a valuable role in the community.

Spiritual Insight on How to Be a Leader

- Leaders are here to serve. It's not about everyone else serving you! Mathew 23:11 says:: "The greatest among you shall be your servant."

- Make sure your heart is right and focus on the mission instead of the position.

- Let Jesus be your example. Follow how He lived and how He treated people.

- Lead others to follow Jesus and not you; remember that it's not about you.

- Recognize the greater call and mission. Leaders are able to build toward a greater purpose and are always focused. They are not worried about the things of this world.

- Be **bold** and unashamed. Leaders don't follow the crowd. They are the light needed to guide others down the narrow path.

Practical Insight on How to Be a Leader

- Share with others what you've learned in life. Don't be afraid or feel like you're *too good* to share.

- Focus on the mission, not the competition. Leaders don't fight to compete; instead, they work together to complete the assignment.

- Take a public speaking class and develop your skill of speech. Use that skill to speak up when it is needed.

- Become involved in a ministry at your church.

- Start a Christian based registered student organization on your college campus.

Leadership Resources

- **Your local church:** Pray and see if God leads you to serve in a certain ministry.

- **The Bible:** Here you will learn the character you need to be a great leader and servant, which is the character of Jesus Christ. Also read about different leaders in the Bible such as King David, Queen Esther, Father Abraham, etc. Leaders weren't perfect, but they obeyed God and had a heart to serve Him and His people.

- **Pinkypromisemovement.com:** To start a Pinky Promise group in your area.

- **Leadershape.org:** Six day intensive program to build leadership skills. Find dates and locations near you.

Young Athlete Exemplifies True Leadership!

Brandi Brown | 22 yrs. old, Australia

Basketball has always been an important part of my life, but when the opportunity for me to play ball in college on a full ride scholarship came, I was mortified. I was about to move from California to Ohio and Instead of feeling determined, hopeful, and excited, I was doubtful and hopeless. I came into my first season a wreck. I begged my parents to let me come home, and I thought about quitting often.

I was miles across the country, I missed my family, and I was experiencing a winter with snow that I'd never witnessed before. I felt alone and basketball was just plain hard. To top off my experience, my team was losing. In fact, during my freshman year, we lost every single game we played that season. We went a perfect 0-31. It was utterly embarrassing.

At the end of the season, I sat down and reflected on everything that had happened. Shuddering at the thought of all the games we lost, I realized I finally had my opportunity to leave. The possibilities were endless. I could get away from Ohio and go to a team with a better record, or I could finally get what I thought I wanted.

Then I thought about the only bright spot of my year. That year, I had become involved with Intervarsity Christian Fellowship/CBC (an on campus Christian Organization) and was immediately overwhelmed by the love they expressed to each other and to me. They believed in me, they supported me, and they saw potential in me that I didn't see in myself. I was led to Joshua 1: 7-9

> [7] *"Be strong and very courageous. Be careful to obey all the law my servant Moses gave you; do not turn from it to the right or to the left, that you may be successful wherever you go. [8] Keep this Book of the Law always on your lips; meditate on it day and night, so that you may be careful to do everything written in it. Then you will be prosperous and successful. [9] Have I not commanded you? Be strong and courageous. Do not be afraid; do not be discouraged, for the LORD your God will be with you wherever you go."*

Listening to God and examining the relationships rooted in Christ that were being built through CBC, I decided that I would stay in Ohio for the next three years. I began to understand that God had a plan for me and that there was a reason that I was there all the way from California, there were things I was supposed to accomplish through Him, and there was a person I was meant to be. I honestly believed that things could better from playing basketball.

God grew my faith like never before in those three years, I became a Bible Study leader in my apartment building; I received evangelism training, and learned what it really meant to be an ambassador for Christ. Most importantly, I learned how to effectively share Christ with my teammates and friends. I will never forget the joy I experienced when my unsaved teammate volunteered to lead our small group in prayer. There were challenges and trials but in my moments of despair, I would always remember what God told me through those verses in Joshua to bring me peace and hope.

On the court, I was learning the value of hard work, how to be a leader, and becoming a better player. Thankfully, we became a better team. My second season, we won 6 games, my third season, we won 10 games, and my senior season, we won 20 games and we finished second in our conference standings. The accomplishments achieved in my senior season were numerous. I was voted Conference Player of the Year, was recognized as an ESPN Women's Player of the Week, broke the schools rebounding record, was a First Team All-American, and was named Honorable Mention All American by the Associated Press. In three years, we went from not winning a single game, to finishing at the top of our competition.

One of the most amazing feelings was giving a speech at my school's annual athletic student awards banquet. At this banquet, I was being honored for the many accomplishments in that year, but it was a blessing to make it clear that all glory and honor was to God.

In the beginning, on my own, many of my doubts were warranted in my own strength. However, in Christ, allowing Him to use me, love me, change me, I had nothing to fear and every reason to be *strong and courageous*. Now, confidently, I believe that He is with me everywhere I go. Upon graduating, I moved to Stockholm, Sweden to play professional basketball and now I currently play in Australia. God has used basketball to move me around the world, and I am blessed to have witnessed God's love being displayed around the earth.

YOU CAN **START A BUSINESS**

In this day and age, starting your own business for many reasons seems like the way to go. With the uncertainty there is now concerning jobs, as a result of the fluctuation of the economy and economic recessions, more people have abruptly lost their jobs. They've been left to quickly search for another job. If they do not find another job in time, then they may consider applying for unemployment and government checks.

According to The Opportunity Nation Coalition, a study shows that "Almost 6 million young people are neither in school nor working" and "that's almost 15% of those aged 16 to 24 who have neither desk nor job" (The Huffington Post). This shouldn't be. The percentage is clearly too high in comparison to the current unemployment rate of over 6% of Americans over the age of 16 (Bureau of Labor Statistics).

I deeply believe that every single person in this world should work unless they're retired. Do I believe that every single person in this world should have a "job"? No. Still, every individual was placed here with a purpose and assignment. Working is a Biblical principle, and it is good. 2 Thessalonians 3:10 says, "For even when we were with you, we gave you this rule: "The one who is unwilling to work shall not eat."

With the special freedoms that we have in parts of the world like America, to implement the visions and dreams that God has given us, there is absolutely no reason why anyone should disregard the option to start a business. I say the "option" because starting a business is not in any way a requirement and I am not telling everyone to start a business. Business is not for everyone and the assignment and passion of many is to join as a part of a larger vision and help build it. I am only suggesting a raised awareness of this liberty that we have in a new world-class economy.

Some believe that they have no option. They have a deep sense of resentment toward the company that they work for and it's simply because, deep down inside, they're afraid to do what God called them to do.

Deferring you God-given-assignment may be detrimental. When you live for Him, you sacrifice all of your worldly pleasures, desires, and fears so that His will is done in your life.

Over a year ago, even before my husband and I got married, the Lord put it on our hearts to start a business and move to Atlanta, Georgia. We did start the business, but we decided to prolong the process of moving to Atlanta because of the fear of what our parents would think about me dropping out of college, and what they'd think of my husband as a leader. Every day since then, the business has been growing, I got married, wrote a published my first book, but I felt an emptiness while in the classroom.

Students would respond to me with contempt when they would hear about my life and see that I was still in school. I'd get comments like, "What are you doing here?" or "Wow, you're way ahead of the game." Not only was it super awkward, but the fact that I was still in school and living a life that glorified God, among many of my peers who were partying and doing their own thing, eventually turned "being a light" into being a "show off". I should have not been fearful when the Lord told my husband and I to move to Atlanta during our engagement. I was prideful because I felt like I had to make something of myself…

for my family and my lineage. I was after success in the world's eyes and after pleasing the world.

Nevertheless, God has been so faithful. I used to work part time at a bookstore for $7.00 an hour. He told me to trust Him, put all of my energy into the business, and He would supply my needs. I never went back to that job and I did as He said. My husband and I have had rough times, but we've grown and all of our needs are met. Not only that, but here and there my husband and I are able to bless others… which has always been a dream of mine.

Now, two months before graduation, I have decided to stop prolonging the process. I dropped out of school. I know that dropping out of school was long overdue, but I would rather be obedient later than walk across that graduation stage with a piece of paper for the man-made approval that God never intended for me to have. God wants to do something different with me. He is showing the world what He can do with a young 21 year old girl, who came from a single parent household, has no college degree, but is a wife, and businesswoman, and servant in His Kingdom. I will not dare to mess up God's plan with my own. May He get all the glory. My husband and I decided one day that we would no longer let fear hold us back in Tallahassee, Florida. Immediately, we packed our bags and left for Atlanta, Georgia. We trust Him to continue to use us in a tremendous way, as He continues to grow our business. Has God told you to leave a place, and do a thing, but you're prolonging the process because of fear?

Being in a job where your life is tied to going in from 9:00 to 5:00 and not having the freedom to: own your own time, spend time with your family, and build your own dreams, can be draining.

Some like the safety and regularity that comes with having a job. Those are, many times, the people who are meant to help build into a larger vision.

You don't have to be in your thirties, married, settled into your career, and with life savings to step out and start your own business. If you're ready, you can start your business now! I've been doing business since middle school, particularly freelance, and I've only grown from then until now.

In high school, I had both business and ministry ideas. Yes, God can inspire you that early. Don't feel bad if the inspiration comes later, but have peace in knowing that His plans are locked into His perfect timing. Wherever you are in life, God has "a hope and a future" prepared for you. That is only one little snippet of one of my favorite verses, Jeremiah 29:11.

Knowing these plans as early in life as I did was great. I haven't had to wait until retirement or old age to see the fruit of my work; I've already began seeing the fruit. Still, even with knowing the plans, I didn't understand the plans or how what the future held would come to pass. I just had to trust in the Holy Spirit, and operate in what I could at the moment. I began doing freelance photography in the tenth grade with the intention of raising donations for an orphanage in Haiti. I had no idea, nor did I have the understanding, of how my photography would later be a tool used in the mission field. But it would, and it is. I started a company called IAMIMAGE and our mission is to inspire people and teach them that they are made in God's image. The thing about being young and doing what God has called you to do is that you have the ability to be flexible, without a care in the world. God loves that. Our lack of attachment to many things, and our novelty to life, makes us more open to being led by God, changing directions, and going with the flow of the Holy Spirit. May God bless even the more, those who choose to drop everything they have during mid life or the latter days. Young people are not the only ones who can have this type of obedience or flexibility, anyone who has a heart for God can. Still, it's something very special that God adores about the younger generation.

I did not have a whole lot of money to get up and fund my business venture when the Lord revealed it to me. But trust me, when the Lord tells you to do something, He will provide a way. I have experienced this provision first hand. With the help and inspiration of the Holy Spirit, I was able to write a business plan of the vision of my photography business/ministry that He gave me. This was years later, toward the end of my sophomore year in college. I applied for a program at the business school in my university called the "Business Incubator". The incubator is an office space with other young entrepreneurs, where you can get your own cubicle and space, access to business and financial mentors, printing, faxing, copying, etc. I submitted my business plan and I was admitted into this program for a year, where I was able to develop my knowledge of business, from marketing, to financials, to human resources, etc. I also received a $5,000 grant to help start my business. It had been five years since I started doing photography and little by little, God was leading me and developing me in fulfilling His purpose in my life. Still, along the way, the mission of my ministry was in effect, even if the vision hadn't manifested into its full potential and season yet. People were coming to realize whose image they were truly made in, not societies, but God's.

Spiritual Insight on How to Start a Business

- A lot of people want to start a business but don't know where to start. They spend hours upon hours researching "get rich quick" ideas and franchise opportunities. These people look at the promise of financial profit down the road and that's the basis of their motivation. Though by their ambition, they are likely to become "successful" as defined by the world's standards, they miss out on true "success".

- The world deems success as a form of social power. This social power is reflected upon financial power and social position—money and attention. Money and attention are not, in fact, "bad". Yet, to base success merely off of social power is very flawed. Those who are truly successful are those who are whole.

- To be whole, you have to be emptied and filled again. You have to let go of the broken parts in you, and stop allowing them to control you. When you're broken, your mind, actions, and, sometimes, even your health are directly influenced by your hurt and can keep you from carrying out your vision in the most excellent way possible, if at all.

- You need to be emptied to recognize the strongest and most consistent parts of you. Brokenness is the fluff that will make your vision cloudy. It's like when you're sad and crying hard and rubbing your tears away, your vision becomes blurry for a moment. Yet, after you finish rubbing your red eyes and crying the tears, just wait, your vision will return clearer than day.

- I'm not saying to forget what has happened in your past. Sometimes, you can't forget. I'm saying, rub those tears away. Don't let them impair your sight and vision. Don't stay crying. Use those tears to pour into someone else's life. Someone is thirsty for your tears. When they come out, they're full of salt and life. The tears from your brokenness can build someone up, if you use them the right way.

- The greatest ideas and inventions come out of places of discomfort, struggle, and strain.

Practical Insight on How to Start a Business

- Develop your idea by writing a business plan. Then be ready for God to tear that business plan up. The business plan is not the end all be all, it's merely a brainstorming tool for the Holy Spirit to speak to you through. Not knowing how to write a business plan is no excuse. I did not know how to write one, so I learned. We have so many resources at our disposal. We have the Internet and public libraries. Make use of these resources. Type in "Business Plan Templates" into your online search engine. Make it a duty to fill in those blanks. If you don't know what a word means, research it. If you don't know the answer to a question, make something up and then when you find out the answer through more research, go back and adjust your made-up answers. Made up information are placeholders but they should be relevant and make sense, even though they may be inaccurate for the time being.

- Investors look for a business plan when potentially funding a start up company. Why? Because most investors are only willing to invest in something that they believe will promise a profit to them in the long run. Or for investors who give out grants, they invest in something because they believe that they are contributing to something that will build the vision of the entrepreneur and further society as a whole. Therefore, a business plan is recommended if you want anyone to take you seriously.

- Research, research, and research your market and other individuals and businesses involved in the same area that you are interested in starting a business. You can learn a lot from those who have been doing this for years. You can also research to develop competitive strategies for your own business, as well as considering different affiliation strategies you can implement.

- Establish your business foundation and create the legal entity.

- Surround yourself with professionals who know what they're doing. Even though you're most likely starting a business because you're passionate about something, generally, there are still many areas that encompass business apart from your passion. Starting a business means considering more than just your craft or passion but the legal, financial, and social elements that surround the core of your business. Become familiar with the proper actors such as: legal practices, terms, lawyers, Certified Public Accountants, Public Relation specialists, Web Designers, Graphic Designers, Wholesale retailers, Distributers, marketing strategists, etc. I guarantee you... you will not know everything.

- Practice communicating your ideas in a professional and efficient way. Develop a thirty second-elevator pitch. Take a public speaking class (research Toast Masters), practice speaking in the mirror, to your spouse, or a close family member or friend. Learn to express your ideas in different and efficient way. Draw them out, sing them, break them down, and share them.

- Protect your ideas with copyrights, trademarks, patents, and discernment.

- Take action to bring your vision to life.

- Master your craft. A lot of times, when we think of an "expert", we think of a professor with a doctorates degree, who has written a book. The truth is, as a young adult, especially if you're living for God… you can master your craft. When you are young, and you dedicate your life to the Lord and truly start living for Him, He will begin to reveal to you your gifts. God is not a respecter of persons (Acts 10:3). He doesn't say, "Well, you're too young, I'm going to give these gifts to the ones who are older, who have been serving me longer." No! As long as you serve God, not matter your age, spiritually or naturally, you are important and have a role to play in the body of Christ.

For example, in Matthew 20, there is the parable about the vineyard workers. A man went out early in the day to hire idle men in the streets work in his vineyard. Before they began working, there was an agreement that they'd receive a penny a day. Gradually, every hour, the household went back on the streets to find more idle men to work in his vineyard. At the end of the day, everyone received the same payment, I penny, both those who had been there from the early morning, and those who had been there for only an hour. Those who had been there since the early morning, started to complain because they felt they had been cheated. Then the householder spoke to one of them and said, "Friend, I do thee no wrong: didst not thou agree with me for a penny? Take that thine is, and go thy way: I will give unto this last, even as unto thee. Is it not lawful for me to do what I will with mine own? Is thine eye evil, because I am good? So the last shall be first, and the first last: for many be called, but few chosen."

God has this same attitude toward the way He gives away salvation and gifts. He gives it to all who call upon the name of Jesus and believe in Him. If someone who was serving God for ten years died in a car accident with someone who just got saved the same morning, they would both have received the same reward of heaven. In the same way, if God does not regard time, but only regards the heart in this situation… what makes us think that He wouldn't do the same for age. God does not care about your age, He is not limited to that. What He cares about is your desire to serve Him, your dedication to using your gifts to bring Him glory. God will have you be an expert in your field, even at a young age. The authority and knowledge you have will come right from the throne of the Almighty.

God can use whatever He chooses to use, to teach you. He will definitely teach you from His word… but He will decide whether or not He wants to teach you from college, or from experience, from the Internet, from books or from all of them together. In this day and age, there are so many different ways to learn and so many resources available to us.

The Holy Spirit has taught me everything that I know, from publishing a book, to starting a business, to understanding His word; it's all from Him. Of course, I had to do my own research as He led me, to sharpen my skills in some areas but in everything, He was leading me and I knew that. I knew that all this knowledge I had been given was not of myself. All these gifts were all from Him and meant to be used for His glory and His glory alone.

Business Resources:

- **Linda.com:** Tutorials and resources on many different business and designer skills.

- **YouTube.com:** You can learn anything on YouTube, take advantage.

- **Library:** You can find books in your library about so many different topics and areas of business. Get a library card and research.

- **Quickbooks.com:** Online accounting and tax resources. I love using this for my business. It's easy and affordable!

- **Paypal.com:** I use Paypal to accept online payments for my business, and then I transfer funds to my bank account. I specifically use a Paypal business account rather than personal account because it comes with many features… such as a Paypal business debit card, a square to take debit and credit card payments when you're out and about, invoice creator, plus you can turn on automatic billing and employee payments.

- **Adobe Acrobat:** So necessary if your business deals with a lot of contracts and you often need e-sign to lessen the hassle on your clients.

- **Creating a website:** It's important to create a landing page for you business online so that customers can access and learn about your business from all across the world!

    - First you need a host: You won't be live on the Internet without a host. They provide the server on which your URL address/website will be.

        - Iamimage.com

        - Godaddy.com

        - Bluehost.com

        - Hostgator.com

    - Next you'll either need a web-designer or a web builder.

        - Wordpress.com

        - Joomla.org

        - Wix.com

        - Webs.com

- **Create a Business plan:** I built mine off of a sample. Search sample business plans online. Find one in your field or niche.

Young Law Student Pursues Purpose

Kyona McGhee | 27 yrs. old, Flint, Michigan

From a very young age, I loved stationery! You know, everything from pens, paper, and notebooks. Anything "memo making related" was basically the best part of my little world!

I know...super random way to start off a story about running a Christian business, but I promise it will make sense in the end! I loved it so much that I begged my mom to get me all paper products and Lisa Frank school supplies for Christmas! I already had it all, but a girl (like me) can never have enough notebooks, highlighters, and diaries!

Because of my love for stationary and everything "bossy" (not the Kelis, version of bossy either) when someone asked me what I wanted to be when I grew up, my answer was always "I want to be lawyer!" At 5 years old, I had no clue what a lawyer did, but I knew they had a huge desk, full of... guess what? All the papers and folders a girl could dream of!

As life ran its course, and the world tainted me, I scaled back my ambitions and I lost faith in myself. I didn't get accepted in to law school after graduating with my criminal justice degree, so I thought it was over. I thought I was going to be working a boring 9-5 for the rest of my life, but thank GOD, His thoughts are not our thoughts!

I had a huge, loud conversation (and by conversation, I mean me yelling, with Him not responding) with God one day because I was so disappointed with barely making ends meet, not to mention not being passionate about my " day job." The very next day I got a call to start working in a field I loved, helping the homeless at a non-profit. This "job" made room for me to hear from God, gave me the time and money to follow anything he placed in my heart, which ended up being *Daughter of the King Royaltee*.

I launched my tee shirt company on Instagram, with no website, no business cards, no business plan, no anything! Just me, God and Instagram! Because of God's leading, we sold over $30,000 worth of tees in our first year! I didn't (and still don't) know what I'm doing. I just follow his lead. My education will tell you I don't belong in this field, but our sales would say different, and I cannot attribute DOTK Royaltee's success to anything outside of God proving that his plans are always greater.

A year into my business, I was accepted in to law school after having never applied again. So of course, I went and stocked up on all the pink stationary available and laughed at how strategic God's provisions for our lives are. DOTK Royaltee now helps me pay for school, He orders our steps, in the order they need to be, not the way we would like them. All we have to do is trust Him.

YOU CAN **BE YOUNG AND MARRIED**

Yes, you can get married young and be happy about it! I am living proof. I got married at the age of 20 and I don't regret it for one second. People have so many reasons for why they think young people shouldn't get married. These reasons include but are not limited to:

- Going to school and finishing your degree

- Being settled in a career and having a large savings

- Living it up before you settle down

I'm sure that the people who make these statements about why others should not get married young mean well, but these statements are irrelevant. They are irrelevant because the very nature of marriage, and its aspect of "forever", says that if we're going to be successful in marriage, we have to been willing to be committed no matter what the circumstance. If you're waiting for the very perfect moment to commit to the "one", or the perfect age or stage of life, you're not ready to be married.

The fun in marriage comes from having the opportunity to grow with your spouse. If everything is perfect when you get married, how will you grow? Here's a secret, even if you try your best to have everything perfect and in place for your marriage, you will encounter surprises, setbacks, and ups and downs. God Himself will send many of these tests… why? For several reasons! God wants you and your spouse to grow and learn together, He wants you to build endurance and cling to your commitment for one another in the rough times. Most importantly, God wants you and your spouse to trust Him. Thinking that you can create the perfect set up for the picture perfect marriage before you tie the knot is boastful.

God creates the perfect marriage when two people who are willing to put Him first.

My husband and I didn't have it all figured out and when we got married we didn't have it all together, either. What needed to be together was our hearts, and commitment to God. In the beginning of our marriage, my husband and I weren't 100% clear on the direction that God was trying to take us in as far as vision. When we got married, I thought I knew the direction we'd be headed in, but our lives went for a turn. I had to learn to step off the scene and release the control so that my husband could lead. When I finally learned how to do this, things gradually became clearer, and before you know it, we shared a solid vision, and we were headed in the same direction.

What was God doing in that situation? God was saying, "Okay, you trust me enough to get married young. I also want you to trust me enough to lead your marriage though you guys may not know everything." This is something Chris and I had to learn on our own, being that all of the married couples we know are a little older and have been through life for quite some time. Still, that is the beauty about being you. God takes you through firsts that other couples don't get to experience. Like the first time one of you receives their degree, or the first time you have to explain to your little kid siblings that ask you cute questions like, "Karolyne, are you an adult?"

"Yes, I am an adult,"

Or when the pre-teen asks, "Do you and Chris live together?"

"Of course! He's my husband" and she runs upstairs… "Mom! Karolyne and Chris live together!"

Many of those firsts are funny, some emotional, and others, priceless. I am so happy I got married at a young age and get to share these moments that wouldn't have otherwise been shared with Chris.

When we got married, we did not have a large savings. As a matter of fact, we did not have savings, period. Can you explain to me how, without a job, we were approved to rent out a two bedroom and two bathroom condo and manage our bills month to month?

Yes, we've had some rough times. We've had the noodles and the peanut butter and jelly. But I never take those moments and say, "Man, maybe we weren't ready to be married." No. My husband used those moments to move our focus toward where God is taking us, and we'd talk about it over our peanut butter and jelly and get excited. We get to go through this together! *Where would I be at the moment if we weren't together? Would I be better off?* I don't consider those thoughts, either. In this moment of marriage to my husband, that will last the rest of our lives, I am only thinking of us, as one, and how we will move forward in our relationship with God on our side.

God has never left nor forsaken us and has been with us every step of the way. He continually teaches us how to manage our finances, and the good thing about being young and making some mistakes in marriage, is that "you're still young." That comes into play and you realize that you have room to work on things.

People think that they're living it up when they're single and dating multiple people at a time, and going to the club, getting drunk. That's whack. You have that one night stand, and never see that person again. Or you have the on and off relationship with someone that always fails. You're fornicating outside of marriage and hoping that it'll fulfill you. The best sex is when two whole people, who are married, become one, and are glorying in God rather than in sin. Sex isn't bad, God created sex. The context in which you have sex is what makes the difference. I was a virgin when I got married to my husband, and I'm telling you, it was the best sex of my life! The good thing about it is, I have nothing else or no one else to compare it to.

You want to live it up with someone else? Living it up that way is a gift that comes within a marriage. Before that, though, you have to be completely surrendered to God. You have to be whole and trust Him to fulfill you. No relationship will fulfill you, not even in marriage, if you do not have a relationship with Jesus Christ. Jesus is the backbone of any young love, or of any love at that.

When my husband, Chris, and I met, we were both living in the world. Even though, up to that point, I had been a Christian for years, as a college freshman, I was going astray to try new things, like clubbing, drinking, etc. Can I just say that there was nothing there but emptiness? I knew what it felt like to be whole, so there was no way I could stay in the lifestyle I was living, and never desire to return to God.

Nine months into our engagement, we knew that we were ready for marriage because we'd never be ready. Our commitment was so strong, whatever could possibly come against us, whether we were ready or not, would not break us. Chris and I were confident that we were able to withstand turmoil and at that point, though you may not know what awaits your marriage in the future, you know that you're ready to get married, not matter what age you are. We we prepared to die to ourselves daily, so that one another could life.

Just by looking over your habits, attitudes, and the circumstances of your courtship, you'll be able to tell how truly committed you are. Are you committed to honoring and respecting your significant other during courtship? Or are you committed to feeding your flesh and giving into temptation? Are you committed to putting God first in your relationship? Or are you committed to putting your own, or your spouses' interests first? The answers to these questions are representations of your true level of commitment. Some younger people are more willing to commit than older people. That is why marriage should not be based off of the level of years you have under your belt, but rather, the level of commitment you have. I am not saying let 5 year olds should get married because they want to get married. With everything comes wisdom. All I am saying is, some of the mindsets that people may have toward young people, or that young people may have toward themselves, should be renewed daily, according to God's word.

At the right time, Chris and I had to come to terms with the fact that as man and wife, we needed to leave the households of our parents, and cleave to each other. In the beginning of our marriage, we were still very tied to our parents, who played a big role and had a lot of say in our marriage. This started to create a lot of arguments between us, and eventually it had to be made clear that the direction we were going in, and the way things were run in our household, would be determined by my husband, and he and I would be the ones to talk about it. If you're young and you feel like the Lord is leading you to marriage, know your responsibility to love, respect, and honor your parents. Still, know that when you do finally tie the knot, know your responsibility to love, respect, honor, and protect your marriage and your household.

Spiritual Insight on Being Young and Married

- Take premarital counseling because you don't know everything. Be open to learning from other godly couples who have been doing this for a while.

- Take post-marital counseling! This is when you'll really have issues to work through.

- Honor God in your courtship by remaining pure and in your marriage by submitting to Him and keeping Him first and He will honor you and your marriage, not matter what age you are.

- Keep God first by not creating idols out of your relationship and pleasing Him before meeting your own desires or that of your significant others'.

- You will continue growing, even within your marriage, so keep in mind, you will never be 100% ready. You don't have to be perfect to get married… just like you don't have to be perfect to have a relationship with Jesus. You just have to be committed.

Practical Insight on Being Young and Married

- Meet each other's friends and family and spend a lot of time with them. If you're trying to get married extra young like I did, there's a chance that your parents may be skeptical of it because of your age. If they don't have a good idea of who this person is they will be even more skeptical and that can cause a lot of drama. The best thing you can do in this situation, especially if you believe that it's someone who God wants you to be with, is to pray and let your friends and family get to know your spouse personally. Make sure your spouse respects you. A respectable thing for a man to do, that the parent should appreciate, is just having a talk to the parent and asking for the lady's hand in marriage.

- Save, save, save for your marriage. Money isn't everything, but always being in debt, never having any food, and rent always being late shouldn't be because of the fact that you made an abrupt decision to get married. Financial irresponsibility can put a strain on your marriage. This is not about whether or not you have faith for God to provide. This is simply about what measures you are taking and what wisdom you are using to truly give God something to work with in your life.

- Keep a schedule to balance out your day when you're married. Put alarms on your phone for everything. If you're going to school, working, taking care of your household, and changing your baby's diaper, you need a way to keep track of all that needs to get done to balance your life and keep progressing.

- Have a plan, especially if you want your parents to support your marriage. It's really not because of your age that they don't want you to get married. It's because they think your age means that you are making irrational and emotional decisions and haven't really taken the time to think things out, which is what a lot of young people do. You don't have to be like that though. You can hear from God, be led by the Holy Spirit, and present a plan of action of what you are going to do to see God's will come to pass in your life. Whatever the plan may be, or how crazy it may sound to others, be open to sharing it with an authority that may doubt your preparedness for marriage. Do you plan on finishing school? If not, why not? Where do you see yourself two years down the road, what vision are you pursuing? They want to know that, and you need to know that.

Young and Married Resources:

- MarriedAndYoung.com: Online community for young and married couples. This online community also has resource materials for single, engaged, and courting individuals.

- TheRobertsLive.com: My husband and I share our journey as a young couple living for God.

- Search: Michael and Amanda Pittman on YouTube

- Youngwifesguide.com: Gospel centered homemaking tips.

Young Wife Chosen to be More than a Bride

Amanda Pittman | 20 yrs. old, Dallas, Texas

My first two years at Southern Methodist University, I made many acquaintances, but I only had two true friends. Robbie, Matt, and I took on the world together. We'd party four times a week, most times, getting so incredibly drunk that we'd laugh at stories we told each other that we'd forgotten of the night before. It felt amazing to be lifted from the sadness of life into a pleasant, light, painless world. Feeling far away from God, the cruise of marijuana was the most spiritual experience I had ever felt. Still in a relationship with my cheating boyfriend, I went to college parties to tease or lead on whoever I pleased. I'd wear the tiniest dresses, the highest heels, and the sexiest makeup. I felt powerful over men, and this gave me worth that neither my boyfriend nor God could give me.

One of the most repelling thoughts of surrendering my life to Jesus was the thought of giving up my boyfriend and my party-girl lifestyle. Every Christian who knew me well enough told me that I needed to leave him, which was too painful for me to bear. Who cared if we resented each other? Who cared if God had a better life for me? How could I give up the very source of my worth?

One night, after partying, I began to cry. I was sad that I didn't feel accepted in college. I wanted to know why others' validation, or lack thereof, only perpetuated my deep-seated, empty void. I pathetically asked Robbie, "Why me?" I had no hope or purpose to live. I wanted validation from others to give my life meaning and worth. I didn't expect Robbie to have anything to say to me. After all, I was too busy drowning in my self-pity to listen. To my surprise, he didn't try to tickle my ears. Instead, with much conviction, Robbie turned to me and said, "Because I think God has a plan for you." It was not Robbie who was speaking—I heard the voice of God.

I began praying a lot. I prayed while I was walking, I prayed while I was working out, I prayed when I was confused, and I prayed when I was excited. The more I prayed, the more God revealed to me. I couldn't get enough of the excitement of becoming co-heirs with Christ, and being unconditionally loved. God was patient. Rather than changing my actions to please Christians, I finally let Christ soften my heart. He embraced me, giving me peace, comfort, and reconciliation for my past, even before my life began to change. As He transformed my mind through the Bible, the rest of my life followed. I stopped drinking at parties, and eventually gave it all up. Because the Holy Spirit was pruning me, the rate at which my maturity grew was exponential. I became so zealous for God's purposes that it no longer made sense for me to be with my boyfriend. I finally felt loved and accepted by Jesus, so why would I want to stay in my unhealthy, draining, unequally yoked relationship? Leaving my boyfriend was the last step I needed to complete to walk into the amazing future God set out for me. I felt so free and overjoyed! I fell madly in love with Christ, and chose to live my life for Him in full.

Immediately, God gave me the love of my life, Michael. Because God placed two powerful warriors together, we then had the capability to touch more lives for the sake of His Kingdom than we ever could have done apart. Michael and I began filming Christian relationship videos on YouTube, writing successful Christian blogs, we've been put in our school's newspaper, have been interviewed for Christian magazines and YouTube series, and have spoken at various Christian conferences. We try to show everyone the love and grace Jesus has extended to us. God loved us so much that, on June 21, 2014, He gave us the wedding of our dreams. We now lead the Young Adult ministry at our church, and pray that God will use us how He sees fit.

I thought that forfeiting my life of crazy nights and hung-over mornings would make me unpopular, boring, or bored. When I put my life in the hands of my loving Father, although, something deeply profound happened. God did not take my life away. I traded in the life I had and Christ gave me a brand new one—a life of abundance, freedom, purpose, and fun. The most thrill and fervor that I've had in life has been through the Christian walk. I gave up the world for Christ because for once, I was accepted and loved. I never chose Jesus because I knew He'd bless me with Michael. I never chose Jesus because I thought I would be able to have a successful ministry. I never chose Jesus because I felt like I deserved His love. In fact, I never chose Jesus—Jesus chose me.

YOU CAN **TRAVEL THE WORLD**

We travel to and fro for many different reasons in this world. With each trip, there is a unique motive and destination. Some people travel for fun, some for leisure, others for change, and others are on a mission. The motives that generally come with traveling make it all the more adventurous. With modern modes of travel, such as car, plane, and ship, traveling happens more frequently and less strenuously than in the past.

In Biblical times, one of my favorite traveler's to look toward, is Jesus Himself. He was a man on a mission, going from city to city, about His Father's business. With traveling, you are apt to meet very different people, in all different walks of life, meaning that you have so much diverse opportunities to leave a lasting impression of hope, on all of the people you meet. I love missions' trips, but you don't have to be on a mission trip to have a mission. I've ministered spoken word in New York subways, when being there on family vacation. You take your mission with you wherever you go, whenever you go. Meaning, I can be on a mission just for the mere fact of traveling to the grocery store, or to school. I may have a mission to share the gospel that day, or a mission to bless someone.

Traveling becomes more fun when you stop waiting for that one-week trip at the end of the summer. When you realize that everywhere you go, no matter the distance, and every day you wake up, you have an opportunity for missions. Missions should be more than your annual charity, if you are a born again believer, missions is your life.

Therefore, look forward toward tomorrow. You are not where God's brought you from, but you are where you are now. There is a reason why you're here. That reason can be a mixture of a few things. Like I said before, people travel with different motives. Life is all about balance. You can still be on a mission while having fun and experiencing change. We travel for many reasons, but at the other side of our destination, someone is waiting for us to meet them. God has placed something in us that was made to encounter them. At the other side of our destination, there is something He is waiting for us to learn. There are people, places, and events, strategically positioned in our lives, to lead us to the final destiny God has planned for us. When God tells you, "go", go. When He says, "Get up and move", trust Him. The plans He has for you are great, and the Holy Spirit is with you, every step of the way.

Spiritual Insight on Traveling the World:

- Make sure you hear from God, before taking a major move in life. You don't want to miss out on what He has planned for you somewhere else.

- Pray before any trip, it is important to be covered before entering any new territory. Pray over yourself, the place where you are going, and the people there.

- When God says go, don't hesitate, and just go.

- Don't worry about the finances if God has directed you to go somewhere. He will provide all of the wisdom and resources that you need to be taken care of.

- Don't become so attached to material things, you need to be willing to let go of all the baggage, and trust in God to sustain you.

- Find a church wherever you go, or a spiritual community where you can stay connected.

- When worse comes to worst, find a church online

- Don't forget your word! You need your Bible with you wherever you go!

Practical Insight on Traveling the World:

- Join a frequent flyer system because you'll save money in the long run by getting to travel more places for cheaper.

- Open your eyes to the opportunities around you. You may not think that you have the money to travel financially but consider these things. Do you still get gifts from your parents and friends on birthdays, holidays, and graduations? Ask for money and instead of spending it on expensive clothes and movies, pay your tithes and offerings and then put that money aside to travel.

- Are you a smart cookie and receive loads of scholarships and grants from your institution? After you pay for room and board, and buy the rented/used books for the semester, put what's left over to the side for travel. Some students think that you can only apply for scholarships and grants when applying for schools but you can continue doing so even after being accepted. Research scholarship search engines online. If you're going for a good cause, you can sign up for one of those online fundraising profiles and ask people to donate to you. .

- Every time you get change back from something you buy or from eating out, put it aside and save it in a travel jar. That change can turn into room service and taxi fees in the future.

- Go with someone else because a lot of times, it's cheaper and most of the time, it's more fun. If you go with a group, you can look into getting group rates for flights or hotel, which end up costing a lot less. Sometimes groups and organizations have their own lodging and meals that come apart of a packaged deal. If you go with a friend, you both can split costs. Someone can pay for all the taxi rides, while the other can pay for all the pizza.

- Search for deals on everything. I like to use priceline.com. A lot of time, simply changing the day of your travel slightly can lower or raise the price. Be sure to study and learn the system. Compare everything to make the best decision. Compare and research different airlines, hotels, deals, days of travel, forms of travel, etc. A plane may not always be the best route to go. Sometimes, taking a bus, or going on a cruise is cheaper and more rewarding in comparison to taking a plane.

- Connect with people before you go because it'll make your travel experience richer and a lot of times will save you a lot of money in the long run. Months ahead of time think of anyone you possible know, who is the closest to where you want to go, or anyone you know who might know someone close to or where you want to go. You may be able to stay somewhere for free instead of paying for a hotel on a tight budget, and get rides offered to you as well. You just have to be open, willing, and connect with others to plan things accordingly ahead of time.

- Always give a gift or thank you card to those offering to serve you as a visitor. Ask them to take you sightseeing or invite them to come along.

Travel Resources:

- **Priceline bidding:** Bid for cheaper flights on priceline.com. Also get all-inclusive vacation packages that come with flight and hotel, etc.

- **Last Minute Cruises:** There are last minute cruises all over the web! Google it. Last minute cruises are very cheap, and cruises are great ways to travel to multiple places on one trip. Plus, cruises are all inclusive because they include the food, travel, and rooms.

- **Mega Bus:** The most affordable travel bus ever! It's a double Decker bus and they have many locations across the US and UK. Bus fares many times are as low as $1 if you get it early enough. The bus has free wifi and is very comfortable for the price. The only thing is, they don't have bus stations, only bus stops.

- **Groupon.com:** Groupon has so many travel deals for groups or individuals. A lot of their packages are all-inclusive and many times may include airfare and meals.

- **Scholarships and Grants:** CAPPEX.com or FASTWEB.com

Young World-Traveler Takes the Nations

— Juliette Bush | 28 yrs. Capetown, S. Africa

I have traveled to 36 countries and have lived in 3 continents. From walking a tiger in Thailand, gliding down the Great Wall in China, elephant riding in Bali, dancing at Carnival in Brazil, making pasta from scratch with the locals in Italy to watching the sunset by the Eiffel Tower in the heart of France. I never dreamed of traveling the world. This dream lifestyle only occurred when I was denied from obtaining my "dream" job.

After graduating from college with a marketing degree and being rejected at every corporate job interview I found myself in, there was still peace in my heart, despite the concerns of everyone around me. A few months later, a friend of mine told me about a job in Dubai. It was a flight attendant position in an international airline, where you would fly weekly to different countries. This is something I never would have considered. I didn't even know where Dubai was! From thousands of applicants, I was one of the few chosen to start this new journey. Little did I know, God had a huge plan for me there that included more than traveling the world.

Living in a new environment and being moved from my surroundings, I began to seek God in a new way. I saw my life in America from a fish bowl. Before, I relied on my pastor to feed me the Word. I didn't seek God for myself. After time, I realized I never had an intimate relationship with Jesus. I said I was a Christian because my family was and I went to church. I didn't read the Bible for myself, therefore, this revelation made me pursue God on my own. I bought a Life Application Study Bible that broke down the scriptures and showed me practical ways to apply it to my life. When I started reading the Bible for myself, life made sense. Each page I turned awakened life inside of me. My desires were changing. I wanted to give into and restore communities for a living. I went to an orphanage in Kenya, where I fundraised for their immediate needs and sowed into their children. I would use my vacation times to look up communities in need to fundraise for them. My next stop was Ethiopia. There, I knew that this is what I wanted to do: be an international missionary. A few months later, I stumbled across a program, where God put it in my heart to do just that. To serve the least of these and build His church. It was a one-year unpaid community outreach internship with a church in Cape Town, South Africa. "But wait, it's not paid. How will I survive?" Immediately, God told me He would provide. My bank account wasn't looking like I could just up and leave to another country for an entire year. I was so scared of what other people would think of me. I just started a blog… I wasn't over my job yet. I was making excuses to validate my stagnation of leaving.

So, I stayed in Dubai for another year. Big mistake. I was no longer graced to be where I was. There was a reason why God wanted me to leave at that appointed time. At the end of the year, I ended up going to Cape Town with less money than I would have had when God originally told me to go. You see, I wanted to make it look as normal as possible, because I just knew people would ask me how I could afford to live without a salary. I wanted to justify my provision because I wasn't secure in my identity in Christ yet. However, anyone could save up money and move to another country, how does God get the glory from that?

I'm so happy that things didn't go my way. It deepened my relationship with God and established my trust in Him as my provider.

On January 27, 2012, I moved to Cape Town, South Africa with just my suitcases and a word from God. All I can say is that God's promises are true and He will never leave you. I am in my second year of living in faith and I have lacked nothing. My core project is developing an early childhood development curriculum that helps to equip moms to encourage their children to reach their full potential. It is an 8-week course that strengthens, equips, and educates families to provide a loving and caring home for their children. Being a part of this initiative has radically changed my life.

God has also led me to a Christian Student Accommodation that has supported my walk and journey. It wasn't the most ideal place for me because it is a hostel and I have lived on my own for the past 10 years, but I laid my desires aside because I believe that God had a purpose for me there. Through staying at the residence, God opened a door for me to lead a Bible Study group in their lounge that has built community amongst the students as well as led other girls to the residence, who have been able to prosper in it's surroundings.

God also put it in my heart to continue blogging and sharing my experiences. Through writing on my blog, it encouraged and inspired three other girls to leave their comfort zone and fly over 10,000 miles from America to Cape Town to do the same internship. Your calling doesn't just affect you, but others around you as well. I have seen these girls flourish in their identity in Jesus and seek and fulfill God's will and purpose for their lives.

My time here doesn't have an end date. I am in Cape Town until God leads me elsewhere. What I initially thought was a "dream" job, God gave me a life that was never in my radar and has exceeded all my expectations. All I said was "yes" and God has been by my side for the rest. I don't know what is next for me, but I know that I am in the path God wants me to be, and He will give me the next step as I follow His lead.

God can do the same for you. You can travel, too. Just go as God leads you. Success is not about accumulation, title, or rewards. True success is living out and doing God's will for your life. When you walk in your calling, you will be living to your full potential, for God has already aligned, graced, and equipped you for such a time as this.

YOU CAN **HAVE FUN**

A lot of times, people wait until they've received a certain age to give their lives to God. They think that surrendering earlier will rid them of opportunities for fun and enjoyment. The truth is, you really start living when you're living for Christ.

The difference between worldly fun and godly fun is freedom. The enemy is an impostor, so He likes to steal God's ideas and those things that are good, and manipulate them. The enemy will have you thinking that getting drunk, having sex, and living recklessly equates to freedom, but it's actually a bondage that has been dressed up to deceive us. We fail to remember all of the consequences that come with living a life of sin. Teenage pregnancies, sexually transmitted diseases, bad hangovers, hurt family members, etc. When you picture the worldly experience holistically, is it really fun? Or is it a moment of fleshy satisfaction in exchange for something more valuable?

True fun and fulfillment will have you covered the whole time, not just half the time. True freedom comes with having peace, when your soul isn't at war within yourself, fighting to survive. We are able to live life to the fullest when we realize that true joy doesn't come from the temporary satisfaction of our flesh, but the eternal position of our spirit. When we are filled with the Holy Spirit, though we may have some rough days, we are still whole in Christ, and don't need to seek others things to fill that empty void inside of us. When we are filled with the Holy Spirit, we are not limited to enjoying our lives on earth, but our joy extends to the spirit realm.

Fun is knowing the God of the universe, and having a relationship with the almighty. Fun is being able to ask Him things that you would never know and having the privilege to hold His secrets and promises given to you. Fun is being able to freely enjoy things within their proper context, such as sex inside of marriage. Fun is being able to see yourself grow, being used by God and seeing Him work through you, to change lives and the world around you. Fun is living a life of suffering in a world full of pain and sin, but still having a purpose and a hope to look forward to.

I am not saying that the Christian life won't have its ups and downs. I am not saying that the Christian life means you will never have to suffer… I guarantee you, you will. But the Bible says, "I consider that our present sufferings are not worth comparing with the glory that will be revealed in us." (Romans 8:18) The eternity that follows this life, if you are saved, will be fun. Singing songs of praise to God and basking in His glorious light… walking the golden streets of heaven to go feast with the Almighty king will be glorious fun. It's a place where there's no more suffering, no more sickness or pain. It's a place where life will never be the same. That is true peace and true freedom; that real is fun. It's fun just to think about it!

What's not fun is being separated from God on earth; being in bondage to sin your whole life, dealing with the consequences of that sin now and forever, and spending eternity burning in hell just because you were so focused on fun, you placed fun over Jesus. Jesus came so that we may have life and that more abundantly (John 10:10). Seriously, why would we pass up on such an offer? Living for God is not a law and you're not "cool" if you break it. Accepting Christ is a gift, and you're missing out if you don't take it.

Spiritual Insight on Having Fun!

- Glorify God in everything that you do, and be happy about it. Try to make Him smile! Use art, dance, music, writing, creation, or whatever it may be to express God's glory through you!

- Be grateful for your life! Be thankful for everything! Having this type of attitude makes almost anything and everything fun!

- Live a life of faith and obedience to God! Disobeying God is no fun because it comes with its consequences… but living a life of faith always brings adventure, joy, and peace!

Practical Insight on Having Fun!

- Surround yourself with a community of believers who are innovative, creative, and love to have Godly fun!

- Become involved with the events going on at your church, and get to know your brothers and sisters in Christ.

- Host a fellowship event yourself! You don't have to wait for an invite; you can be the life of the party!

Fun Resources:

- **P4CM.com:** Christian Spoken word poetry events and videos.

- **OneGodUnited.com:** Christian event organization of America.

- *101 Other Things to Do Than Have Sex, Hump, Bump, and Grind:* Book written by Jennifer L. Tyler to help promote abstinence in relationships.

- **Christianconcertalerts.com:** Lists the dates of all Christian concerts nationwide.

- **Events and socials** hosted by your local church and the Christian organizations you are involved in.

Young Sorority Girl Finds a New Way to Party!

Alisha Willis | 23 yrs. young, *Odessa, Texas*

I've been in the exact place you are in. I thought life was just about going to parties and doing whatever pleased my flesh, no matter the physical, emotional, or spiritual cost. I had no conviction about any of the sins I committed. I disobeyed my parents, I lied to get my way, I had no respect for myself, and I ran to the things of this world to satisfy my every need. As a result of this mentality, it lead me to heartbreak, an abortion at the age of 18, depression, and just feeling that there was no way I could ever stand before Jesus and believe that He would accept me just as I was. I was a mess!

I thought Christians just went to church all day, every day and practically had no life. Although I was never a drinker, I was worried about what my friends would say if, all of a sudden, I started refusing to go to the club or refusing to hang out in places that did not glorify God. I even questioned if I would still have those friends. I questioned what I would do on Saturday nights if I didn't go to the club. I'm in a sorority, so I was expected to be at all the parties and clubs. I did not want to be at home by myself on a Saturday night.

However, I began going to church and surrounding myself with a community of believers. I had to choose to get out of my comfort zone, which was, and at times, still is, a struggle for me. As a result, they began inviting me over to their houses on Saturday nights to just have girl talk, eat, laugh, watch movies, etc. I soon realized that this was the type of community and friends I had, deep down, been longing for. The club satisfied my worldly desires, but deep down, I knew I didn't belong there. I knew I belonged around a body of believers who were more concerned about my eternity than my worldly pleasures. Was it easy? No! I lost a lot of "friends", but I was so determined to live for Christ.

In that process, I gained sisters who love me, encourage me, and want the absolute best for me. As my relationship with God grew, I no longer desired to go to the club. I traded the club for quiet time with Jesus and fellowship with other believers, and it has been one of the best decisions I have ever made. God met me where I was, all I had to do was cry out to Him! Be open with God. Tell Him your fears and concerns about giving your life over to Him. Tell Him that you don't want to be bored with your Christian lifestyle. He'll honor your transparency and send you some of the most fun Christians you'll ever meet. It'll seem like there's never a dull moment with them. However, it takes time. Just like any other relationship, you must communicate and be open with God, spend time with God and read the Word so you can learn what pleases and honors him. It's a process, but it is so worth it!

PART 3:

Examples from the Past and Present

LETTERS ABOUT **THOSE WHO DID**

The following letters are about young men and women of the Bible who God used to do mighty things in the earth realm and further His will and purpose. I pray that you are encouraged as you read about those who already DID what we are raising up again to do, as a young generation, boldly living for Christ.

Young Jesus Was About The Father's Business

When Jesus was 12 years old, His parents found Him teaching in the temple. According to the bible, He was sharing great knowledge with doctors there. I think it's funny that Jesus was speaking to "doctors" and answering their questions because these days, it seems like one of the biggest oppositions to Christianity is science. At a young age, Jesus knew the answers to many of the questions that we don't even know today. It says in Luke 2:47: "And all that heard him were astonished at his understanding and answers."

His parents were looking for Him and the bible goes on to say: "And when they saw him, they were amazed: and his mother said unto him, Son, why have You done this to us? Look, Your father and I have sought You anxiously. And He said to them, "Why did you seek Me? Did you not know that I must be about My Father's business?"(Luke 2:48-49)

At a Young age, Jesus' parents were "amazed" by His walk of faith, but they didn't fully understand it all the time. Sometimes God will lead you to do something and live a life of faith that your parents just wont comprehend. That shouldn't deter you from doing God's will. Of course we are still subject to our parents when we are young, single, and living under their roof, but remember, God is and will always be your first parent and first priority. That is why I love that Jesus says He is about His "Father's business." He understands that honoring His parents means honoring God.

Young David Conquers a Giant

David, the youngest of eight sons, the son of Jesse, was chosen by God to become King over Israel in place of Saul. David was the one who stepped up to the Philistine Giant, Goliath, and saved Israel from becoming slaves to the Philistines. He also eventually led the Israelite army to many other victories. When God chose David for this, he was only a humble shepherd of his father's flock. That should serve as a reminder of how us young adults can be used by God, especially if we have proven faithful in the little things first. (1 Samuel 17)

When God sent the prophet, Samuel, to appoint David as the future new King, Samuel was taken aback to realize God's choice, but the Bible says in 1 Samuel 16:7, "But the LORD said to Samuel, "Do not consider his appearance or his height, for I have rejected him. The LORD does not look at the things people look at. People look at the outward appearance, but the LORD looks at the heart."

What I love about this verse is that God said He rejected Him. Isn't it funny how God can choose you, work through you, but, at the same time, make you a reject? Not a reject to Him, of course, but a reject to this world. God does that on purpose, so that we may be a light and His glory can shine through us.

Young Mary Bears the Savior

Did you know that Mary, the mother of Jesus, was a young woman? At the time, in Israeli tradition, the Rabbis set the age of marriage for younger women at twelve years old. The men, though married at older ages, found younger women to marry. In Isaiah 7:14, Mary is described as a "chaste virgin". She was a devout believer and servant of God. God chose Mary to carry out his will and birth the baby Jesus, our Savior. (History's Women)

If God could trust even Marry, to play a significant role in His plan to save the world, what makes you think that He won't use you?

Young Josiah becomes King

According to 2 Kings 1:1-2: "Josiah was eight years old when he became king, and he reigned thirty-one years in Jerusalem. His mother's name was Jedidah the daughter of Adaiah of Bozkath. And he did what was right in the sight of the LORD, and walked in all the ways of his father David; he did not turn aside to the right hand or to the left."

God is the one who chooses Kings and those to put in authority. If He put King Josiah in charge of *Jerusalem*, a major city of the time, than what makes you think that God wouldn't call you to be in charge over something important? God isn't worried about your age; He is concerned with your faithfulness.

I love how it says that even at that young age, King Josiah "did what was right in the sight of the Lord." At such a young age, he had discernment and knew the difference between right and wrong. So what is our excuse? We know what's right and we know what's wrong but we choose to act as if we do not. The Lord is going to choose those young people who proudly embrace His word and His ways to carry out His mighty plan.

Young Timothy sets an Example

Timothy was the young pastoral assistant to the apostle Paul. Paul was so proud of Timothy's faith in God at such a young age and gave him advice on how to train the teachers and pastors of the time. Paul wrote to Timothy, in 1st Timothy 4: 11-12 and says: "Command and teach these things. Do not let anyone look down on you because you are young, but set an example for the believers in speech, in conduct, in love, in faith, and in purity."

Many times people will look at the young and make instant judgments about them. They may say, "Oh, they're a babe in Christ" or "Ugh, they're just so immature" but physical maturity has nothing to do with spiritual maturity. Some young people may actually be more spiritually mature than those who are more physically mature in stature and in age. That is why Paul tells Timothy, "Don't let anyone look down on you because you are young, but set an example for the believers." He said "set an example for the believers" because a lot of this judgment, comparison, and hierarchy unfortunately happen in the church. Could it be that God is using young people to defy the odds and break that churchy attitude?

When Paul is speaking to the church in Corinth, He also goes on to say: "Brothers and sisters, I could not address you as people who live by the Spirit but as people who are *still* worldly—mere infants in Christ. I gave you milk, not solid food, for you were not ready for it. Indeed, you are still not ready" (1 Corinthians 3:1-20). The very fact that Paul had to use the word "still" shows that he is talking about those who have been in the body of Christ for a while. In that case, He was generally speaking to those who were physically older but spiritually remained as babes in the church.

We can encourage growth in the body of Christ by being fully transformed at our young age. Meaning, we shouldn't only say we go to church, but our actions should match our confession, as we bear the fruit of the spirit. That is what is means to be an example.

Young Gideon Conquers His Enemies

God called Gideon, who was the least in his Father's household, to save Israel from the Midianites. At first Gideon was afraid, but God assured Him that He'd be with him. In Judges 6:16 it says: "And the Lord said to Him, 'surely I will be with you, and you shall defeat the Midianites as one man." God was to be glorified through Gideon's victory, so he made him get rid of almost his entire army before going into war. His army went from 22,000 to 300 men. This way, everyone would know that the victory would have happened no other way besides the favor of God. God was with Him, and he did as the Lord said. For that reason, they won the war.

When God decides to use you, especially when you're young, He may tell you to get rid of some things in your life so that He can get the glory. I dropped out of school two months before graduation, at the leading of the Holy Spirit. Many make think I'm crazy, but faith doesn't make sense…it's not supposed to make sense. How do you think Jesus fed five thousand people with only five loaves of bread and two fish? It was by faith. "And without faith it is impossible to please God, because anyone who comes to Him must believe that He exists and that He rewards those who earnestly seeks Him" (Hebrews 11:6). Could it be that, rather than being justified by a degree and people believing that my success is based off of that piece of paper, God wanted to do something different? Maybe He wants to get the glory for all my success. Everything comes from Him anyway.

Young Samuel Listens to God

From the time that he was a mere boy, the Lord spoke to the prophet Samuel. He informed Samuel of the judgment that was to come upon the house of Eli and the bible says in I Samuel 3:19: "So Samuel grew, and the Lord was with him and let none of his words fall to the ground."

You don't have to reach a certain age or a certain social class for the Lord to speak to you and tell you His secrets. If you are truly willing to listen, and obedient to speak when God tells you to speak, your relationship with God can be such a powerful tool for the Kingdom!

Young Esther Becomes Queen

I love the story of Esther. Esther is a great role model for young women in the body of Christ. She was virtuous and beautiful on the inside and out. King Xerses had a rude, nagging, and ungrateful wife named Vashti, so he decided to replace her with a new queen. According to Esther 2:8-9,

> "When the king's order and edict had been proclaimed, many young women were brought to the citadel of Susa and put under the care of Hegai. Esther was also taken to the king's palace and entrusted to Hegai, who had charge of the harem. She pleased him and won his favor. Immediately he provided her with beauty treatments and special food. He assigned to her seven female attendants selected from the king's palace and moved her and her attendants into the best place in the harem."

Esther not only became queen, but she also had a purpose during her reign, she saved the Jews from being annihilated by a devious man named Haman. Despite her youthfulness, Esther displayed a great example for the other women in the Kingdom to look up to. She was loving, submissive, and had a gentle spirit. She not only had favor in the eyes of the King and the people in the city, but also in the eyes of God.

LETTERS FROM **THOSE WHO ARE**

The following letters are from youth and young adults who have accepted Jesus as their Lord and savior and have dedicated their lives to being a light for Him. They will share their testimonies of how they were saved and explain why their desires for God are so strong as opposed to desiring the things of this world. They were once where you may be. Do not hesitate to pull from them, any piece of encouragement needed to get you to where you need to be.

Young Woman Discovers a New Love

Alyssa Harkness | 27 yrs. young, Kennesaw, Georgia

I want you to ask yourself something, *What if I spent all this time and energy on the wrong road, pursing the wrong things?* I asked myself the same question a couple of years ago. *Could I dare to be different? Could I give up trying to conform to what society said I should be? What would it cost me to conform or not to conform to the world?*

These questions were weighing on my heart and mind right before I spoke with my "sorta-kinda" ex-boyfriend. Right before I cut it all off... for real this time. I was sick and tired of selling myself short. I yearned for more, and my ex wasn't it. I refer to him as my "sorta-kinda" ex because we had entered into a sorta-kinda relationship. You know, the one... *when you're in town, I exist... when you're not in town, I don't exist.*

I grew up knowing of God and sometimes going to church. My parents are still married and my dad has always been involved in my life. No dramatic or traumatic events of my youth. So, what led me to decide to be in this relationship? And how did I get out?

Basically, we were young and I was looking for a "happily ever after" type of love. Something like, *"College sweethearts, falling in love, getting married"*...yes, that story! I didn't think it was a big deal that we weren't in a committed relationship. I thought, *maybe he needs time... just not now... it's okay that no one knows about our relationship, except the people who I told,* which was a big mistake!

I was trying so hard to conform to the things that pleased him. The more and more I did, the more and more I neglected my family and close friends. I looked myself in the mirror one day and I realized I had become that girl who went to church every now and then, and was involved in a Christian organization, Pinky Promise, but I still gave more of myself to him. I was so sad and depleted of energy. I started to ask myself, *How did I allow this? Is this all I was worth? God! There has to be more!* I had never felt so much peace after saying that! Literally, I was in my apartment and I said this aloud to God. He put on my heart the most important decision I had to make. *Everything I desired and needed hinged on this.* I knew that after 3 years of this nonsense, I had had enough! I was ready to accept whatever challenges came my way. Only because God was leading me and giving me the tools and skills I needed to do work.

So, I called up my ex and the conversation we had was very peaceful. Before calling, I prayed for strength, the words to say to him, and that I would control my emotions, no matter how he reacted! He respected my wishes to stop seeing one another. He also said, *"Well, you know, if you ever need, you know, me to come by…just call."* My response: *"Uhm, no, sir, I'll be good."* We said goodbye. I deleted his number and blocked it too. Since that time, I haven't tried to call or email! Yes, the urge has come, but thanks to God, I passed those tests and didn't reach out to him! I haven't dated anyone, either. I have remained celibate for close to two years now and am waiting on God's best for me to begin a courtship.

My life now has totally transformed. My relationships with my family and friends are much closer. I am back together with my sisters in Pinky Promise (they are awesome; they prayed for me during this time).

Now, please understand, this road, being a true Christian, has had its tests and trials, God said it would. But, I wouldn't trade it for the mess I was in before!

I'll leave you with this- know that your story, your testimony, is yours! How you accepted Christ and started living for Him is real. For some folks, it happens in church, or riding in the car with their family, or like me, in your apartment or room! Jesus has never left you, He is always there holding your hand...He is constant, consistent, and persistent.

So, rest assured, He will help you along this walk. He is waiting for you. It's worth it! *Christ met me in the mess I created and He will do the same for you!*

Young Author Shares Her Life Transformation

Andrea Wyche | 23 yrs. young, Hampton Roads, Virginia

I didn't grow up in church. When my older sister was of age to drive, we started going to church together often. I continued to go even through college. But there was something missing. There was no change in my life. I would go and then return to doing exactly what I was doing before. I never really had anyone explain to me what it meant to be saved. I was baptized when I was 12 so I thought I was good until I realized that there just had to be something more to this.

The church I was going to was a mega-church. I showed up every Sunday and there were all these new faces and no real relationships were formed. Service was exactly 1 hour and 45 minutes long every Sunday. I started going to a new church that was very small in size but the warmth I felt when I walked through the door was like none other! I finally felt like I belonged somewhere!

One night after Bible study, the mother of the guy who I was seeing at the time, asked if it was okay if the elders of the church prayed for me. My response was, "Sure!" No one had ever laid hands on me and prayed before. They circled around me and anointed my head with oil. They prayed about issues they couldn't have possibly known that I was dealing with. I fell to my knees and cried out to God! I needed Him and now I knew! I accepted Him into my heart on that night. I was 20 years old.

Going to church only on Wednesday for Bible study turned into requesting to work a later shift so I could attend church on Sundays. My change had come! To understand the depth of this change, I have to go back to high school.

Throughout high school, I dealt with depression, even cutting myself for a period of time. I was in a 5-year relationship, where I allowed myself to be cheated on and treated horribly and then I, too, became a cheater. I had a low self-esteem and did not know my worth. I got drunk and partied on a regular basis. I stole often just for fun. My freshman year of college, I went through a period of depression again until I transferred to a new school. Even still, I cussed recklessly and spent my weekends drinking and partying with friends, fornicating, lying, and did whatever else I wanted to do. Long story short, I was a wreck!

God can change years of being a mess in such a small amount of time. When I talk to people about the old me, they can't even believe it! I tell them that it is completely God who changed me! When I wake up in the morning, I am so thankful for this new life in Christ! In the two years that I have been saved, I have experienced trials but I can honestly say that this life in Christ just keeps growing sweeter and sweeter.

I have accomplished things I never even imagined I would do. In 2013, I asked God what my talent or gift was and He showed me that it was writing! Something that I have always loved to do! I started a newsletter at my church called, "The Water Weekly" and have written 26 issues. In February of 2014, I published my first book, *That Long in Your Heart: A Study Guide for Young Ladies Searching for More*. The fact that I could use my own life experiences to encourage and inspire other young ladies is amazing. I have also had the opportunity to speak at a youth event and will be on a panel of an awesome women's conference this year! Oh, and the guy who I used to "talk to" in my past, also was saved in 2012 and we got married July 5, 2014! It was so much more meaningful on our wedding night because we had both been abstaining from sex. No matter what you have done in the past, God can and will use you when you make the decision to live for Him!

Young Wife is Delivered From Past Hurts

Angel Jackson | 22 yrs. young, Washington, DC

As I walked down the aisle, I felt all of my baggage falling off. The weight of carrying depression, suicide, low self-esteem, and all of the emotional damage of being molested at the tender age of 12, began to hit the ground with every step I took forward. When I reached the altar, I began to pour out my heart to God. All of my hurt, issues, anger, and bitterness were now being presented to the only one who has the power to heal such things. I felt the warm embrace of Jesus overtake me as I accepted Him into my heart as my Lord and Savior at the age of 16.

Since that day, I have been boldly living a life for Christ! Yes, I have fallen short, and I have made mistakes, but God's grace has kept me! Looking at my life now, I can truly see how far God has brought me. Before I was saved, I was a broken little girl who felt abandoned, worthless, and all alone. Even after I was saved, I still faced many trials and tests. A year after I was saved, I was raped by my then boyfriend. That tragic event turned my world upside down. I was in such shock that I tried to convince myself that it didn't really happen.

I waited 3 months before I told my sisters, and I never opened up my mouth about it to the rest of my family members. I was "saved", yet I was so bound. God had to completely expose me to my own self. I had to admit what I was going through, and tell God how bad I was hurting. It wasn't until I was honest with God and myself that I was actually able to truly experience freedom in Jesus! As unworthy and as undeserving I am, God loves me unconditionally! He loves me in spite of my failures, and it's only by His love, grace, and mercy that I didn't take my own life, but chose to give it to Him instead.

Today, at 22, I am blessed to say that I have grown tremendously since the age of 16, and I am continuing to grow each day. I have the honor and privilege to be married to my amazing husband, Joshua, and the mother of our beautiful son, Joel. I am currently a proud stay at home mom, who is constantly working to be a better wife, mother, daughter, sister, servant, and friend. I have a passion for writing poetry and natural hair. I love to inspire other, and help people walk in deliverance and freedom. I know that I have been called to be set apart, and I have fully embraced my purpose in Christ. I thank God that I gave my life to Him at such a young age, because I could be living a completely different life right now, or not living at all.

Young Writer Shares the Hope of the Gospel

Ann-Sophie Ovile | 20 yrs. young, Haiti

Before salvation, I didn't know what Christians meant by being "saved". I was just living my life, saying that I loved God but doing all of the things of the world. The truth is, I never asked myself if God was pleased with my actions. When you don't fear God, you never really ask for His opinion. God doesn't even cross your mind before you act. You just do it because you simply feel like doing it. This makes all the difference between being saved and living in the world. When you accept Christ in your life, you will know that He is with you at all times and you will care about His opinion. Suddenly, some things will not feel so right.

I remember when some songs started to bother me. I had listened to them my whole life, and suddenly, all the lyrics sounded so wrong to my ears. Jesus saves my friend. He will come and clean you from the inside out. He will help you clean your atmosphere. You will have new playlists, you will read new kinds of books, and it might be scary at first but don't resist the change. Change is painful sometimes but not as painful as staying the same when you know who God created you to be. The old life doesn't make sense anymore once you know the truth.

Make the first step, open the door, let His love invade your space, let it invade your life, and you will discover the meaning of pure happiness and pure freedom. Jesus has the power to break your chains if you let Him in. He will not only break the chains you knew you had but He will also break the ones you had no idea about. These are the most dangerous chains. It might be something you settled for. Maybe you grew up with no money, so now you think that you will never prosper because your family has always been poor. Or maybe it's about marriage. Because everyone in your family is getting divorced, you think that marriage makes no sense; you think that love doesn't exist. Maybe it is about success. No one graduated in your family. Where you come from, it is rare to graduate so you think that you will follow the path. Maybe it's about sickness. In your family, people always get sick, cancer, lupus, scoliosis, you name it, and they have it. So you think that it is normal for you to get sick, too. God wants to break these chains in your life. The invisible chains the devil uses to keep you in a cage.

He paid the price of your salvation. All you need to do is open the door of your heart and recognize that you need Him in your life. Don't resist the call. Be part of the army who is rising up for the Lord. He wants to use you, don't resist. He will find you. Just call Him. Only when you will fully accept who you are in Christ will you be able to embrace your purpose. Don't listen to the voices keeping you from moving forward. If you are reading this today, it is for a purpose. It means that a part of you is crying out to Him, asking him to show you a way to keep walking with confidence. I am here to tell you that it is well in Jesus name. In my book, *Daughters and Sons of the King*' coming out on January 16, 2015 God inspired me to write for all of those searching for a way to get back to Him. I pray that reading it will inspire you.

Young Daughter of the King Shares the Truth of Eternity

Domenica Kary | 21 yrs. young, Shreveport, LA

Being a child of a king requires so many rules to be followed, restrictions not to exceed, and some boundaries never to be crossed. How will we ever get it right? At least those are things I thought when I first decided to follow Christ. Those thoughts and questions are purely opinionated, and have little to do with the character of God, and everything to do with the character of the individual exclaiming them.

When you're on the front side of change, it's hard to see things for what they really are. We will never be able to see things the way God does. Before giving your life to Christ, you may be accustomed to doing things your way with no care or concern in sight, but in the process of deciding to give your life over to the One who can truly care for it, you begin to see things such as His protection, over your life as restrictions, removal, and restraints from the things you think you want.

All these thoughts stem from your character and when you begin think as such, you begin to assume the task before you is too challenging. Do not run from the challenges presented to build, grow, and nurture your character. You're okay, it's just a process, and it's pushing your faith beyond its normalcy.

We all want to get it right and no individual has it perfected, so we all must continue striving. If you are thinking you still have more life to live before you surrender to God, I am asking, "What if you don't?" What if you die tomorrow? Every young person says they want to "live their life to the fullest", but as a 21 year old, live-spirited, energetic person, who can't resist a good "turn-up", I wasn't *truly* able to start living my life to the fullest until I gave my life to Him.

See, I knew I was a bit too careless about where my future was headed, I was a little on the reckless side. I needed someone who knew how to *properly* care for me even when I didn't know how to care for myself, and Jesus was exactly that for me.

When you give your life to Christ, it is not the end of living your life to the fullest; it's actually just the beginning. Christ looks at your heart; He sees the purity in your intentions even when others can't. I gave my life to Christ long before I had changed my living for Him. People make you believe that when you surrender your life to Christ, the next day or week you will be walking and talking completely different, like a one-week makeover. That is *not* true! Realistically, the same night you give your life to Christ, you may have the same thoughts as the night before you gave your life to Christ, but your *reactions* to those thoughts should now be different.

People will tell you that living for God will be an *instant* life altering moment. They are correct about it being a life altering moment but *"instant"*, not so much. Every habit you engage in has been learned through repeated involvement, so as you begin living for God and learning more about Him and the characteristics of Him, some things will steadily begin to change. Even after all you have done, God can still use you. There is purpose in every struggle you've encountered and every mistake you've made. The more you study about God and discover how amazing He is, some things you will no longer participate in, not because the desire for it is gone, but that desire for Him has increased and you now care more about His image than your own. Notice I spoke a lot about what *"people say"*, because the biggest demolition you can do on your building process whether believer, or non-believer, is being moved by the antics and/or opinions of *"people"* who are imperfect, yet trying to find their way just as you. These *"people"* often have demons that are working to keep mask so they will pick at your flaws to keep attention off of their own.

Stay connected to people who are further than you, people who are striving to reach similar goals and have similar plans in mind. Learn from them, grow with them, and pull from each other's strength. Trying Christ should never be looked at as an experiment; it's nothing short of an amazing experience.

Young Child of God Finds the Peace She's Always Longed For

Ivie Erediauwa | 21 yrs. young, Nigeria

I wanted to be a Christian who lived for God but I wasn't ready for the sacrifices I'd have to make. I wasn't ready to displease people to please God and I definitely wasn't ready to die to the desires of my flesh. So I continued living for *me* and somehow, I was getting by.

Then I hit rock bottom. I was tired of feeling frustrated and incomplete. I wanted that constant nagging feeling of inadequacy to disappear for good and I let God know that I was for real this time.

He asks those who are weary and burdened to come to Him and He will give them rest (Matthew 11:28). I was desperate for rest; I just wasn't sure how to leave the lifestyle I was so used to. How could I *not* be friends with these people I had known forever? What would I do for fun? What would people say about me?

God in His infinite wisdom knew that I'd ask these questions even before I formed them in my head. Not only did He place people with the exact same goal I had in my life, but He began to give me a kind of peace I can't really explain. So what if people spoke about me anyway? I was living my life for Him and no one else. All of a sudden, I just wanted to make *Him* proud. I wanted people to associate me with God and not the world. It doesn't mean there aren't moments when 'the world' seems more appealing, but that is why I rely on His strength and not mine because in those moments of weakness, His strength is really made known (2 Corinthians 12:9).

I truly believe that it is all about your desire. It isn't about what you show the world or the number of hours you spend in church. It's about the number of hours you spend alone with Him in your room. It might seem like nothing is happening, you can't hear His voice and you feel exactly the same, but believe me, God is working on you. All you have to do is hold on long enough to see it.

Now, I have peace. It is by far the greatest gift I've received since surrendering completely to Him. Life with Him really is something. I am so confident in His love and His promises to me. I believe that He loves me with every fiber of His being. All He wants are repentant hearts that are surrendered entirely to Him. Since this truth became planted in my heart, my life really hasn't been the same. I now know that when I slip, it doesn't make me a sinner, unlovable or unredeemable. Why? It's because my Daddy is eagerly waiting for me to run back to Him with a repentant heart. He doesn't hate me and He hasn't condemned me (Romans 8:1). He is so faithful.

I won't sit here and tell you that life has been perfect since I surrendered my life completely to God but I can assure you that it's nothing compared to life before Him. I still fall short, but the peace and certainty I have in Him cannot even be put into words.

Young Student Finds Her Strength in Christ

Sierra Sutton | 23 yrs. young, Maryland

One special accomplishment in my life was graduating from college. The summer before my last year at Towson ended on a bad note, or so I had thought. That summer, my boyfriend and I decided to end our three-year relationship. I was so distraught; my mind couldn't fathom life without him. Not only had our relationship ended but the summer was almost up and my financial aid didn't come through.

That summer, I felt God leading me back to the church I grew up in. I knew I couldn't go back to my boyfriend's church, where I was attending regularly because my focus would be tainted because of our faltered relationship. So even by the first service I attended, I knew God was speaking to me. Toward the end of the sermon, I heard God say, "Don't worry, I've got him", speaking of Jordan. I never opened myself up to love unconditionally as I did with him and I didn't want to let go. So at the end of this service, there was an alter call. It was a while before I approached the altar as the elder pleaded that God was waiting on a specific individual. When I stood before her, she confirmed that it was me.

I immediately let go of my anxieties, worries, and fear about Jordan and school and placed all my trust in God. Then I was submerged in His Spirit. This was the most amazing feeling I've ever experienced. It was unexplainable, nothing on this earth felt better than what had happened to me at that alter. I felt accepted, loved, complete, and free. I felt like I finally belonged, something I desired my entire life. After the service the elder spoke with me, and she asked about school. I told her I didn't know if I would go back because of financial aid but she assured me that I would graduate. Sure enough, financial aid came through. God moved so quickly, I was in awe!

Fast forward toward the end of my final year; four months before graduation, I found out that I was supposed to register for graduation during the fall semester. So I explained to admissions that I never received an email concerning registration. Come to find out, an email wasn't sent to me because I didn't have enough credits. I'd been going over my transcripts with my counselor because I transferred and this never came up. Frightened, I sought guidance from admissions and my counselor, only to end up with the advice to test for the credits. Meanwhile, the test was expensive and I didn't have the money to pay for it. God instructed me to review my transcripts. I went over it multiple times and found that my previous school didn't transfer one of my classes. I contested and this process took a couple of weeks and all glory to God, I was cleared for graduation.

That year, I felt so lost and alone but God saw me through. He provided me with wise counsel, peace of mind, and an abundance of comfort. God let me know that He was my sustainer, provision, and protection. I decided to give God my heart and my desires. I said, "Alright, God, if it's for me then it won't change." I gave God that relationship and my academics because I made an idol out of both. I let life's cares take the forefront and God was not pleased. I realized that I would be okay, regardless of my relationship or degree status, but without God, nothing could move. God turned my whole sense of thinking around. When I relinquished my desires and concerns to God, He provided a way for me to graduate but most importantly, He filled the void in my heart.

Young Lady Finds What She's Been Missing

Terrenique Bastian | 21 yrs. young, Nassau Bahamas

"I have a lot of time to change my life, I have to make the best out of it first" This was always my defense to why I wasn't ready to be a Christian. In my eyes, the life of a Christian was lifeless, dull, and lacked excitement. I grew up in a church home and was always conscious of God but I ran from fully surrendering to Him because I was convinced that the Christian way of life was only for old, traditional people.

My brain was programmed into thinking that I had all the time in the world to change; there was absolutely no need to rush! I agreed to have all the fun I could possibly have and then when I reached a decent age, and was ready to settle down, then I'd invite Jesus into my life. I wanted to experience life and have some "fun" while I was still young! Simple as that!

I had a burning desire to fit in and be accepted by the crowd, I watched closely as my friends and everyone else around me enjoyed this exuberant life that was so tempting, and, inch by inch, it began to lure me in as prey. I ran with the motto "You only live once" as I plunged into a world that introduced me to vulgar passions, reckless behavior, and selfish motives. I felt right at home! I was captivated by the fast life and loved living life on the edge! I finally got to do things my own way and didn't think I needed a Savior.

I was having fun; everywhere I walked, I turned heads and received the attention I was desperately craving. This life was exactly what I anticipated it to be, but I still had problems that needed to be resolved. I turned to the clubs to dance away my troubles, in hope that they wouldn't return. I tried to block out everything that was hurting me, turning to the wild partying and drunken nights numbed the pain for a while but after the party was done, I still felt like something was missing. I lived with this hollow pit in me for quite some time and I couldn't figure out why I always came up short. Until I realized that the "high" I got from the world was only temporary and could only fill that hollow pit for a short while.

The Christian life is not what most people perceive it to be! This decision was the best I've made! Christianity is not a boring lifestyle; it's what you make it! It's your choice if you want to be a dull Christian. There are a plethora of things you can do while being a Christian, you're free to travel around the world, go cliff jumping, hang with friends, have Bible-study sessions, go on movie dates, laugh, and the list goes on.

The only difference is your focus is now fixed toward living for Christ and you no longer partake in those actions that bring about eternal destruction.

> "The acts of the flesh are obvious: sexual immorality, impurity and debauchery, idolatry and witchcraft, hatred, discord, jealousy, fits of rage, selfish ambition, dissensions, factions and envy, drunkenness, orgies, and the like. I warn you, as I did before, that those who live like this will not inherit the kingdom of God." (Galations 5:19)

After all the "wild fun" and senseless drinking is done and the party's finally over, somehow, you still end up short and hopefully, you realize that something is missing. Take a dose of Jesus, He's the only cure!

Young Beauty Queen Gains an Eternal Crown!

Joann Eneita | 22 yrs. young, Nigeria

In 2010, I took part in a beauty pageant to represent my university out of 50 other universities in Nigeria. At that time, I wasn't saved. I was deep in the world and so filthy. I thought it was like every other pageant but I was wrong. When I got to camp, it was more like a Church conference. I felt like I was in the wrong gathering and could not believe I would be spending the next three weeks there.

Every morning, afternoon, and evening, we were fed daily with the word of God. We had fasting and prayer sessions, we had a deliverance session, praise, and worship. One day, the organizer of the pageant called me for counseling and he told me that I was holding on to something and that I could never move forward in life until I released forgiveness to a man who sexually harassed me when I was a little girl. I sat there, thinking, *How can I do that? Forgive? Not me! I want to kill him when I find him, you can't tell me who to forgive or not.* I was so broken, I cried and wept. He told me that unforgiveness is a destiny killer. I got on my knees after resisting for so long and he prayed with me.

I finally forgave the man from my past and I felt so light and so peaceful. The next day, during one of the Bible study sessions, there was an alter call. I responded to the call and surrendered myself to God. I begged Him to heal me of all my demons and cleanse me of all my sins. I was made whole. I could not wait to get home and tell everyone how I found the One who has saved me, picked me up, cleansed me, and still called me His own.

I didn't want the crown anymore because I had the *best* gift, the gift of *salvation*. I called my mother and begged her not to be upset if I don't win anymore because I had gotten more than the crown could ever offer me. Little did I know, it was only the beginning of my new life. The final day came and my family traveled to come watch their me perform. The contest started, and I made it to the Top 10 out of the 50 ladies that we competing. I could not believe it! I was thanking God on stage (because, I was the 1st in my university to make the Top 10 in this 4th edition).

From the Top 10, I was called to the top 5. I was so surprised! The strength, wisdom, boldness, and confidence I had that night was the Holy Spirit. It was time to announce the winners after our talent performances, the runner ups were called out, which left me and one other contestant, I was on stage but my mind was not there, when I heard the other lady being called as the 1st runner up and everyone was screaming and running toward me, I wondered and looked! I was the winner! I won! I was crowned the queen! I broke down crying. Out of 50 beautiful and intelligent girls, God's grace was upon me. Not by my power, nor my might, but by the Spirit of God.

It didn't end there, I had the opportunity to tour around Africa, I met and dinned with Presidents, Senators, Governors, Ministers, etc. I had the honor of representing my country, Nigeria, and God. God not only crowned me but He healed me. After sixteen years chronic asthma, fourteen years of short sightedness, two years of hipbone dislocation, I was fully healed and whole. Drugs and surgery are not what healed me but it was God. He has not stopped blessing me. Even to this day, as an ex-queen, I am still invited to camp to share my story and testimony with other queens and God has been using me to touch lives and pull them back to Him. I am 22 years young now, and I have *never* seen a better yesterday. I have been surfing on waves of Glory. God is still the same, yesterday, today, and forever... ever ready to surprise and favor those who choose to serve Him, and crown them with an eternal crown of life!

Young Jewel Finds Her Truth Worth

Zakisha Gordon | 24 yrs. young, Louisiana, USA

My early teenage years were full of hopelessness and uncertainty. I struggled on a consistent basis with who I was. Even though I had a pretty good head on my shoulders academically as well as athletically, I found myself engaging in things that proved that I truly didn't know who I was, let alone who I belonged to.

At a very young age, I was molested by some family members. Being exposed to that carried over into my teenage years, where I started to believe that allowing boys to have sex with me was the normal thing to do. I thought this was the way to show love and to experience how much someone really loves you.

Years passed by and it was the same behavior of getting into relationships and having sex while deep down knowing that there had to be more to a relationship than that but at the time, I wasn't exposed to the truth of Jesus Christ. I longed for something greater.

One weekend, I decided to go to an encounter retreat at this church I had been visiting for a while. During this weekend, we weren't allowed to have any kind of electronics so that we can focus on God. This is the weekend I found out about the love of God and how He allowed His only son to die on the cross for my sins. I remember the feeling like it was yesterday. I felt renewed, restored, and honestly, I felt brand new.

I remember leaving the church with a fire down on the inside of me. I felt like I had the Holy Ghost fire deep down in my bones and I wanted to feel more, I wanted to know more about God, and I wanted to experience Him on another level. Jesus has saved me and I knew that without a doubt I had been changed.

I began to tell everyone about my experience with God. No matter what I go through now, I know that God love me and I can reflect on the time that He saved me when I was a teenager. When situations arise in my life and attempt to weigh me down, I can stand firm knowing that God has brought me from a long way. He has brought me through some things that the devil could have used to destroy me but I thank God for His grace, His mercy, and His forgiveness toward me. Now I have every reason to smile because I know who I am in God. "I praise you because I am fearfully and wonderfully made; your works are wonderful, I know that full well" (Psalm 139:14).

Young College Student Discovers the Permanent Void Filler

Tiffany Gregory | 23 yrs. young, Atlanta, Georgia

There is a reason as to why you can't give up the clubbing and drinking; most likely, it's the same reason you began clubbing and drinking in the first place, to forget and/or numb some type of pain you are experiencing. I would know, I was not happy my first few years in college. I was stressed because of grades, work, life back home, and my up and down relationship with my boyfriend. Alcohol quickly became my friend, with partying and smoking becoming a close second.

I knew God did not want me doing what I was doing, but I just could not face Him or the pain. Growing up, I was taught to be strong; to keep it moving and to do what you had to do. So instead of just dealing with years of hurt, anger, frustration, and loneliness, I just chose to forget about it, at least for a couple of hours. My mantra was: out of sight, out mind, and out of mind, out of life.

There is a pain and a void lurking somewhere deep in your heart that you think can be filled up with alcohol, parties, sex, and drugs. If you were truly happy with your life and living it up to the fullest, why would you drink so that you could forget parts of your life and take away from those "happy moments"? Why are you trying to add more to an "already full" life? It's because you're not happy and you're not living life to the fullest. Trust me, I know because I've been there. A lot of people thought my life was going pretty well because of what I would post on social media sites. That is exactly what I wanted. I wanted to convince these people that my life was amazing, because I truly felt it wasn't. What people on these sites didn't see was that while I was capturing, posting, and savoring these few fun moments, I was getting drunk and high to forget the more frequent bad moments.

When you're so full of something, you don't have a need or room for anything else. This is only possible with Jesus Christ. He becomes your source of joy, peace, and contentment. He the most permanent void filler, unlike the partying and alcohol that fades the moment you wake up the next morning. You see, these things are like vapor, they are there one moment and gone the next. That is why you desire to refill yourself with these things and get addicted to them. Yet, our Heavenly Father is like a well that never runs dry. Once He fills you up with His Holy Spirit, you'll never become empty again… unless you decide to pursue sin again. But then again, once you've truly tasted and seen that the Lord is good, you'd never want to be without Him!

Made in the USA
Lexington, KY
22 November 2014